D1604021

Darker than Blue

The W. E. B. Du Bois Lectures

ON THE

MORAL ECONOMIES OF

BLACK ATLANTIC

CULTURE

Darker than Blue

Paul Gilroy

The Belknap Press of
Harvard University Press

*Cambridge, Massachusetts
and London, England*

2010

Library of Congress Cataloging-in-Publication Data
Gilroy, Paul.
    Darker than blue : on the moral economies of Black Atlantic culture /
Paul Gilroy.
        p. cm.—(W.E.B. Du Bois lectures)
    Includes bibliographical references and index.
ISBN 978-0-674-03570-6 (alk. paper)
    1. Du Bois, W. E. B. (William Edward Burghardt), 1868–1963—Political and
social views.   2. African Americans—Politics and government.   3. African
Americans—Civil rights.   4. Liberty—Political aspects—United States.
5. African Americans—Intellectual life.   6. United States—Race relations.
7. United States—Moral conditions.   8. Consumption (Economics)—United
States.   9. Human rights.   10. Geopolitics.   I. Title.
    E185.97.D73G56   2010
    973'.0496073—dc22   2009022179

This book is dedicated to the remembrance of

St. Claire Bourne and Hiram Bullock

We are poorer without the fruits of their
cosmopolitanism and their creativity.

Contents

Darker than Blue

Introduction

These chapters were originally presented as the W. E. B. Du Bois lectures at Harvard University. Ten years elapsed between the original invitation to participate in that series and the eventual delivery of my manuscript. I felt honoured by the opportunity afforded me in Du Bois's memory and wish to thank everyone involved in it, particularly Professors Skip Gates, Tommie Shelby, and Werner Sollors. In preparing these chapters for publication I have attempted to preserve their spoken quality. They do not pretend to be complete statements of a programmatic kind. I hope they will be received in a similarly heuristic spirit to the one in which they were offered.

I hope also that this book is not judged to be solely about the fading political voice of African American popular music. That would be an interesting and timely topic, but my ambitions for what follows are rather more broad. I was keen to make some conceptual suggestions that might contribute to a necessary revitalisation of African American studies during a critical moment in its history and to bring that beleaguered field into a new dialogue with some more recent academic and political initiatives.

The lectures represented my attempt to awaken a different understanding of Du Bois's intellectual and political legacy than has become conventional. For him, the color line was a social and historical rather than an eternal phenomenon. We, on the other hand, are beset by economic and ecological crises, chronic neo-imperial warfare, and a raging argument over the status of human rights. This situation places African American studies under intense pressure. The field's traditional, vindicationist habits are clearly insufficient. What would the sage of Great Barrington have said? If the precious institutional gains of the civil rights period are not to wither away, their academic defenders cannot afford to remain sequestered in the old comfort zones. The students we teach and hopefully inspire will have to be able to address uncomfortable and difficult aspects of contemporary political and economic life.

I suggest that a self-conscious process of updating, deprovincialising, and rethinking could begin by focusing on three sets of issues. In all of them, the politics of race and racism, as well as the political and commercial value of blackness, have been altered decisively. Those key areas can be loosely identified through, first, the problems arising from an unsustainable consumer culture; second, the adjustments following from the contestation of human rights; and third, the geo-political conflicts that have appeared with an apparently endless info-war in which African American cultural "software" now circulates as generic Americana.

That inventory constitutes the context in which I propose an urgent reconsideration of the changing place and value of black Atlantic cultures. This operation must negotiate the tension between, on the one hand, a unique, world-historical culture of freedom which was initiated during the overthrow of racial slavery, and, on the other, its more dubious contemporary traces. Lately, some of them have acquired high visibility as an adjunct to various commercial processes and high political value as diplomatic assets of the United States in a global counter-insurgency operation.

The idea that there are moral dimensions to the black Atlantic's heritage of freedom struggles supplies an initial way to approach this complexity. Those evolving moral aspects are examined here through a critique of the dimensions of contemporary U.S. culture which associate personal freedom with private automotivity. They emerge in somewhat different relief as part of a consideration of the distinctive reflections on the idea of human rights that were articulated in successive battles against slavery and racial hierarchy. Last, the black Atlantic's fading freedom culture and advocacy of peace are considered through their embeddedness in the geo-political dynamics of the long "war on terror."

1

Get Free or Die Tryin'

Now to talk to me about black studies as if it's something that concerned [only] black people is an utter denial. This is the history of
Western Civilization. I can't see it otherwise. This is the history that
black people and white people and all serious students of modern
history and the history of the world have to know. To say it's some
kind of ethnic problem is a lot of nonsense.   —C. L. R. James (1969)

The geo-political order is changing. Old inequalities persist and new
varieties of unfreedom emerge. The racialised structuring of our world
which was established during the nineteenth century is evolving too.
The north Atlantic no longer lies at the centre.

This situation requires new analytical tools and conceptual adjustments. The scale on which analysis operated previously has to be altered
in order to take emergent patterns into account. The teleological sequence that made the overdeveloped countries into the future and their
formerly colonised territories into the past is being left behind. If the
West now represents the past while the rest are to be the future, what
does that change do to the assumptions about history and historicity
that were required by racial hierarchy?

Economic crisis has meant that the analytical approaches which made African American studies, and African diaspora studies more generally, into an academic presence must also be reexamined. The increasingly global character of the political economy of new world black cultures evident during recent years did not foster interest in the operations of the capitalist system or in the spread of African American cultural forms. This silence reflects the fact that those hard-won scholarly initiatives were devised in a different era. Their various intellectual architects were practitioners of vindicationist and insurrectionary approaches which had been shaped by phases of capitalist development earlier than the one we currently inhabit. Whatever political orientation they assumed, those activists and institution builders resolved the complex issue of capitalism and its relationship to racial divisions in a simple manner. This was usually done either by pursuing the expansion of African American access to capitalism's bounty or by dreaming of the system's overthrow. In both cases, the interpretive significance of slaves having themselves once been commodities was set quietly aside. The incontrovertible humanity that was sought in opposition to the racial coding of the world was not recognised or explored as a negation of the reification which the slaves—no longer infra-human objects—had overcome.

Inside the United States, the culture of freedom which had been the slaves' gift to the world was not endowed with historical significance beyond the various phases of reconstruction and the formal award of political rights. After the Hegelian and Marxist imaginings of figures like W. E. B. Du Bois and C. L. R. James, the idea that the slaves' pursuit of human freedom could retain any broader philosophical, political, or commercial importance was seldom considered seriously.

Whether capitalism was to be rendered inclusive or overthrown, nationalists and vindicationists alike accepted markets as an essentially natural arrangement that worked according to the specifications of orthodox economic theory. If the influence of Marxism was intermittently strong, so too was the impact of a Victorian ideology of uplift which acquired distinctive, U.S. flavours. That particular way of thinking about status, property, race, and nation circulated worldwide as an important element in the earliest, generic forms of a black politics that had begun to spread during the inter-war years of the twentieth century. Significantly for my purposes below, nationalistic faith in self-elevation was not the only response to the challenges of that period. The pursuit of civil and political rights generated complex reactions against the lingering imprint of racial slavery. That movement, like the organisation of colonial peoples towards their independence, devised and projected conceptions of human freedom which were incompatible with racial hierarchy, wherever it was located. This was a universal, human freedom quite different from the freedom to consume that the evolving capitalist market afforded slave descendants by way of distraction from and compensation for a wider inequality.

Apart from the battles for human recognition and political rights, black vernacular expression sought and found new freedoms in areas of social life that were not readily amenable to the tempo of lawful and respectable commerce: in the vitality of no longer abject and exhausted bodies; in sexual, familial, and household life; in linguistic play and cultural *style*; in the larger health of a public world which was not simply the opposite pole of a closed and idealised, bourgeois privacy; and last, for a few, in the very ideals of that bourgeois privacy which supplied an index of social advance as potent as it was deluded.[1]

The same period saw the culture of freedom which had been rooted in overcoming slavery become a powerful political force far beyond the borders of the United States. Corporate and commercial interests based there gradually colonised that special formation and severed it from the historical conditions in which it had been created. In due course, its residual force would not only help to condition the dynamics of global commerce as a process of Americanisation, but would effectively supply a compelling signature for U.S. culture worldwide.[2]

Elements of that history and its consequences for analysis of the political cultures and economies of the black Atlantic are explored below. I consider aspects of what it seems appropriate to call—following Edward Thompson—the "moral economy" of black Atlantic culture.[3] I do this not to downplay the fundamental significance or scope of political economy, but to contest the limited place provided in that paradigm for questions of morality and political culture. Those components of social and economic interaction lie at the heart of the critique of consumer capitalism and its freedoms which supplies my initial focus.

The antagonistic view of capitalism ventured here not only departs from the idea that African slaves were once traded just like any other commodity, but also tries to invest the modern history of commerce in human beings with an analytical significance which is alive to the possibility that it still has ethical implications for the present. Though, in recent years, the capitalist market has contributed some of its own special energy to battles against crude racial hierarchy, there is nothing either automatic or permanent about that fortuitous connection.

Thompson was interested in the political culture of the eighteenth-century poor, which he accessed through an exploration of their riotous struggles over the very essentials of life during the revolutionary shift from paternalist to free markets. I want to borrow some of his political nous but to combine it with different interpretive tools drawn from other experiences of exploitation and powerlessness, and then to address the result to another history of dissent and accommodation that might counterpoint and even extend his inspirational narratives of *class making*. I'll try to fold the results of this combination back into a counter-history of the modernity that culminated in the political cultures of the postindustrial poor inside the overdeveloped countries. In particular, I want to consider some of that group's many struggles over elements of life that, when compared to the bread sought by Thompson's mobs, must be judged emphatically inessential. The fleeting things that have captured their attention may involve human dignity, but they are only rarely a matter of life and death. They exercise ephemeral attractions in a society in which consumerism has largely superseded the rights and responsibilities of citizenship, and in which politics itself affords few meaningful possibilities for either redress or progress. In that ignoble, postmodern space far removed from the imperatives of scarcity, the roles and sensibilities of the citizen and the consumer are often set firmly against one another.[4]

As this unsustainable arrangement took shape, racial differences not only became integral to the processes of selling and advertising things—they helped to name and to fix various products in an elaborate system of racial symbols.[5] Inert objects were infused with the vital power to identify, communicate, and even to produce the particularity of racialised groups, assisting their transitions into political and social actors.[6] In other words, what might be called racial identities were sometimes composed by complex attachments to varieties, brands, styles, and objects of consumption.[7] Initially these psychological, cultural, and economic relationships included varieties of food, clothing, music, and sport. Eventually, as the technological framework for these encounters expanded to include digital media, glamour and bodily vitality itself would be added to the list of things that could be acquired in the marketplace.

As part of his pursuit of the new, alternative humanism which characterised his early work, Frantz Fanon described the formation of racial ontologies as part of the sociogenesis of deeply alienated human subjects. He was primarily concerned with the phenomenological apprehension of racial objecthood by racism's victims, but his repeated references to the grinning *nègre* who looked out, wide-eyed, from the French advertisements for the tropical drink Banania suggest that he had started to grasp the significance of consumer culture as an epoch-making context in which the Negro appeared not merely as an object, but as "an object in the midst of other objects."[8] A racialised and therefore necessarily abbreviated (Fanon's term for this would be "amputated") conception of human subjectivity had been manifested in the twentieth-century dreamworld of a consumer culture which was not, at that point, fully saturated with contending commercial possibilities.

In that economy, the images of black celebrities and sports personalities began to acquire commercial value. Jesse Owens was, for example, an early recruit to the cause of selling Coca Cola worldwide.[9] The pluralisation and patterning of markets along racial lines and the tailoring of specific products to particular appetites were the outcomes of this phase.[10] Blackness, which for so long had been entirely worthless, could be recognised as becoming endowed with symbolic value that nobody appears to have anticipated. Needless to say, new forms of racism emerged with these big developments. As Fanon's pioneering efforts reveal, some challenging assertions of irreducible human sameness can be found in this conjuncture. They were voiced in explicit opposition to racial hierarchies.

Whatever was going on in Martinique and Paris, African Americans were being interpellated as consumers long before they acquired citizenship rights. Those two contrasting opportunities to demonstrate their freedom, one political the other commercial, became entangled. There is evidence to suggest that, at times, forms of conspicuous consumption contributed to the strategies that the minority pursued in order to win and to compel recognition as human beings, as fellow citizens and as Americans with a profile that belied the lowly, racial specifications of foolish, childlike negrohood. In certain circumstances, owning or being seen to use the right object could include or support the anticipatory actions performed by these would-be humans as their inconceivable humanity was placed provocatively on display.

Black Markets

The social and commercial processes involved in the passage beyond scarcity and towards citizenship did not just foster the development of markets for things like race records, ethnic entertainments, or the famous Madam C. J. Walker's celebrated "Hope in a Jar" cosmetics—that is, for commodities that were designed to appeal to black consumers. Those processes also included transactions in blackness itself. That variety of exchange was part of a symbolic system which would become increasingly transnational in character. These market relations exceeded the limits put in place successively by the racialised origins and/or attachments of their various participants. A layered and subdivided marketplace, overflowing with seductive new products, conflicted with the disciplinary forces which set out to regulate the rigors of a racially segregated and stratified society.

Gradually, it became possible for some of North America's racial inferiors to buy and to enjoy things that they were not supposed to have. Indeed, forbidding legitimate access to those desirable objects often made them all the more attractive. Rendered valuable, and employed as a medium that transmitted the pleasures, dangers, and opportunities of transgression, blackness could be offered slyly to whites as well as blacks. Its double appeal should be seen in the historical context created by emergent consumer culture and the social and political forms which corresponded to consumerism while racial segregation endured.[11]

In 1932 Paul K. Edwards, a professor of economics at Fisk University and a Harvard MBA, published *The Southern Urban Negro as a Consumer,* a detailed and sophisticated study of Negro market behaviour. His extensive data encompassed issues like credit risk and diet, as well as his subjects' degree of attachment to the branded goods available at various price points; their reactions to the appearance of menial Negro types in advertisements; their newspaper-reading habits, and their economic patronage of their fellow African Americans, which was apparently born from a growing "race consciousness." Three years of extensive fieldwork in twelve southern cities included contact with "white business communities" who had developed a "keen interest in the Negro market."[12]

The commercial and scholastic inquiries initiated by Edwards would emerge again in an intensified form once the struggle for civil rights was under way. Writing in the *Harvard Business Review* in 1961, Henry Allen Bullock described a great prize awaiting the sellers who could approach a Negro market of seventeen million people via an "integrated" advertising strategy. He described the desire of advertisers to reach that new market, their need to know exactly where consumer behaviour might diverge along racial lines, and their evident reluctance to assume that the different racial groups might be similar. Racial differences in consumer activity sprang, he argued, from contrasting reactions to the psychological force of "belongingness." "Negroes want group identification, [whereas] whites, feeling that they already have this, want group distinction." More cryptically, he continued: "Since they [Negroes] have not been allowed to swim in the mainstream, they have been forced to make the eddy waters of American society their own private swimming pool."[13] A case study of contrasting approaches to the purchase of automobiles formed the spine of the article.

A lot of the marketing literature that followed these breakthroughs expended considerable energy on debating the existence of a Negro market and grasping its characteristics as a technical problem for advertisers rather than as a social or cultural one. How, for example, did the roles of the department store and the shopping catalogue vary between blacks and whites? Was telephone shopping a "nonstore" option for Negroes? How far would they travel to shop? Would they use their cars to get there? Were the differences in consumer behaviour detected between blacks and whites consistent at all income levels?[14]

In the mid twentieth century, exercising the franchise was still only a remote possibility for many people, however black political culture had begun to change in this new commercial environment. Political outlooks were being reshaped by patterns of interaction in which racialised subjects discovered themselves and their agency through their social life as consumers rather than as citizens. Many African Americans formed and signified their solidarity through objects: finding and los-

ing themselves as they moved through an ever more commercially saturated space from which politics would gradually be evacuated or in
which it would be allowed to degenerate. The racial community's journey toward human and civic recognition involved the retreat of publicity and the privatisation of their culture. Neither of those outcomes has
been addressed with sufficient clarity by historians so far.

Fanon had appreciated the way these changes were being registered
even as they began. His view of the resulting complexities became clear
even from Charles Markmann's inappropriately Americanised translation: "I was responsible at the same time for my body, for my race, for
my ancestors. I subjected myself to an objective examination, I discovered my blackness, my ethnic characteristics, and I was battered down
by tom-toms, cannibalism, intellectual deficiency, fetishism, racial de-
fects, slave ships and above all else, above all: 'sho' good eatin.'"[15]

Railroad Cars and Private Cars

Moving across this historical terrain requires that we proceed carefully
and in the illuminating company of W. E. B. Du Bois. He was a theorist
and interpreter of African American experience for whom the compromised *public* space of the Jim Crow railroad car provided a central topos.
In that absurd location, official, legal segregation touched and debased
the worthy lives of black America's mobile, modernising caste. Seated
there, the sublation of their freshly doubled consciousness was something they could begin to imagine.

The *private* car—so important to the civil rights struggle and indeed to
the status inequalities which prepared the political way for it—was an altogether different matter. Its unique, dizzying freedoms have proved
more enduring, more immediately satisfying, and more potent than the
merely political varieties that supplied the first and last focus of Du
Bois's analytical scheme and lasted through to the boycotts of public
transport that defined the goals of civil rights struggle and fixed the mythography of Rosa Parks's historic, freedom-hastening bus journey.

Parks's refusal has rightly acquired an elemental force. It counterposed the humiliations routinely found on public transport with the liberty and autonomy of individualised automotivity which allowed the boycott to be successful after the segregationist authorities had put the squeeze on Montgomery's Negro taxi companies. Martin Luther King himself revealed that a pool of some three hundred drivers had supported the boycott by moving the elderly, infirm, and isolated into and out of the city with "military precision":

> While the largest number of drivers were ministers, their ranks were augmented by housewives, teachers, businessmen, and unskilled laborers. At least three white men from the air bases drove in the pool during their off-duty hours. One of the most faithful drivers was Mrs. A. W. West. . . . Every morning she drove her large green Cadillac to her assigned dispatch station, and for several hours in the morning and again in the afternoon one could see this distinguished and handsome gray-haired chauffeur driving people to work and home again.[16]

This networked combination of actors and objects requires us to abandon the standpoint afforded by Du Bois's segregated railway carriages, and with them any residual anxieties over how long the evening train's been gone. We must turn instead towards the automobile, which will function in the argument that follows as a kind of *ur*-commodity lodged at the meeting point: the crossroads of moral and economic relations. The private vehicle tunes us in to the new conditions characteristic of consumer culture. It provides a means to investigate the moral economy in which, as we witnessed in the aftermath of Hurricane Katrina in 2005, the value of life is persistently specified along racial lines and car ownership remains an unspoken prerequisite for the exercise of substantive citizenship.

In thinking about the different histories of automotivity that arose in

France and the United States, Kristin Ross identified the fundamental significance of the automobile in sustaining a transformed relationship between production and consumption: "The car *is* the commodity form as such in the twentieth century, an argument that becomes all the more convincing when we remember that 'Taylorization'—the assembly line, vertical integration or production, the interchangeability of workers, the standardization of tools and materials—'Taylorization' was developed *in the process of producing* the 'car for the masses' and not the inverse."[17] These observations suggest that the problems precipitated by the revolution in automotive technology and its accompanying commercial transformation cannot possibly be reduced to their impact on the social lives of African Americans. Tom McCarthy, a historian of automobile culture in the United States, does not address the specific significance of the car in a racially segregated social order, but his useful analysis endorses the idea that envy, status, and class-based forms of conflict—between urban and rural, as well as between rich and poor—were important parts of the decisive impact cars made.[18] We can extend these arguments by looking at how automobiles acquired a particular significance in the context of the U.S. racial nomos—a legal and spatial order—that secured segregation and promoted the reproduction of racial hierarchy.[19]

Given the epoch-making social and commercial impact of the automobile, there have been surprisingly few discussions of cars in histories of black Atlantic and African American vernacular cultures, political mentalities, and freedom aspirations. In African American history, the motor car and the social and cultural relations it created and reinforced are—as in much twentieth-century social science, even in those specialised studies that purport to address space, public culture, and city life—rapidly passed over, naturalised, or simply ignored.

My argument aims at more than a reflection on those missed opportunities. It begins by pondering the uniquely intense association of cars and freedom in black American culture and suggests, first, that the motor car is a far bigger issue than historians of the black vernacular and subaltern social life have let it become. Second, I argue that analysis of the lives of African American communities and their broadest political and economic hopes cannot avoid taking automobiles into account. Third, I suggest that an assessment of how these groups have responded to and participated in consumer culture is overdue and that the automobile supplies the best tool for all attempts to understand both their behaviour as consumers and their diminishing distance from citizenship. Recently, the geo-political issues arising from the need to ensure secure supplies of petroleum for the United States have added another dimension to that discussion. Discrepancies in the consumption of energy and the political economy of oil contribute to a planetary divide between north and south which cannot be easily separated from considerations of neo-colonial ambitions and resurgent imperial domination over areas that enjoy significant oil reserves. This has serious implications for any approach which would align the struggles of U.S. blacks against racial hierarchy with wider movements to decolonise the world and to set it on a more sustainable and equitable economic path. In view of those developments, we must be prepared to ask whether new insights might be gained through a better understanding of the special, symptomatic points where cars have acquired a symbolic importance far beyond their material and even political currency.

Once we learn, for example, that African Americans spend something in the region of $30 billion on cars and $9 billion more on related products and services, and that they constitute roughly 30 percent of the automotive buying public although they are currently only 12 percent of the U.S. population, it is difficult to resist the idea that the special seductions of car culture have become an important part of what binds the black populations of the overdeveloped countries to the most mainstream of dreams.

The data on African American consumption of automobiles is contradictory and has not as yet been subjected to a detailed historical periodisation.[20] I propose a critical approach to it tentatively, as a reluctant driver who was perplexed by the distinctive social relations produced in the United States by belligerent corporate and governmental manipulation of the global market in petroleum, by the lobbying power of oil companies and car manufacturers against public transport, and by the capacity of the auto manufacturers and distributors to address their black consumers through a curious blend of separatist and nationalist rhetorics laced with the routine themes of what we should probably call American automotive utopianism.[21]

One small but interesting clue to the historical and sociological puzzles these developments produced may lie in the fact that the vernacular speech of African Americans still sometimes refers to automobiles as "whips."[22] The term suggests that deeply repressed and fragmentary acknowledgements of the painful slave past may be quietly active, undergirding the patterns of sometimes ostentatious and excessive market behaviour associated with black consumerism in general and the African American desire for automobiles in particular.[23]

Let me emphasise that the pursuit of a critical angle on the history and sociology of African American consumerism and car culture does not mean that I play down the continuing force of the U.S. racial nomos. The relative poverty of African Americans and the contemporary entrenchment of their segregation and their lack of equality have resulted in lower overall levels of automobile ownership than those found among whites. However, those who do have a vehicle are more likely to have a luxury model and to have spent a higher proportion of their income on purchasing it.[24] I am not inclined either to ignore the sharp class divisions inside African American communities or to minimise the authoritarian force of the stern obligation to drive and lead a driving life which is their nation's civic signature. From my perspective, those important factors make the enigma of African American automobile consumerism all the more profound. It is therefore important to underline that this eco-political speculation over aspects of African American consumption does not pretend or aspire to be an analysis of African American consumer behaviour as a whole.

My concerns are of a more restricted order, and I can clarify them with the admission that they have been provoked not only by my distaste at the apparent triumph of antipolitical and assertively immoral consumerism in black popular culture, but by a range of commentaries on the meanings of automotivity in U.S. culture and the complex and difficult relationship between race hierarchy, automobiles, and freedom in post-slave culture and society. These attitudes were exported to black communities in other areas of the world, along with the generic versions of black political culture that followed the demise of Black Power.

One obvious, notable example of their global reach was provided by the landmark Jamaican film *The Harder They Come* (1972; directed by Perry Henzell). This innovative movie was important in the marketing of reggae as a global commodity. It did a great deal to create the coffee-table exoticism that enshrouded that music with an exciting aura of Caribbean danger and tropical transgression which made it attractive to rock audiences. The film includes a brief but telling scene in which its antihero, the celebrity gunman Ivan, goes to an elite tourist hotel presumably to enjoy a bit of the high life that has been denied him by his sufferer's lot as an inept hustler in the gullies and shanties of Kingston. We see Ivan, smartly dressed, leaving the building, and as a uniformed commissionaire holds the door open for him, the outlaw is enraptured by the arresting sight of an expensive white convertible. He reaches intuitively for its radio but he cannot actually drive the vehicle. In obvious need of a chauffeur, he briefly kidnaps the hotel's doorman, who drives him off to a neighbouring golf course where he gains control of the car and enjoys a hasty joyride among the tees. These wordless scenes are accompanied on the soundtrack by an ironic excerpt from the film's famous title song. The doomed Ivan appears ecstatic behind the wheel. Driving the expensive convertible seems to fulfill his fantasies of opulence, comfort, and freedom. In the context of absolute poverty, that ecstasy may be even more insidious and toxic than the recurrent images of cowboy gunplay that Ivan has absorbed from the cinema and that get replayed as he meets his own end at the hands of the soldiers who have been despatched to kill him. Like the spaghetti western that inspires his own pathological bravado, Ivan's racialised romance with the car can represent the intrusion of Americana into circumstances so inappropriate that it can only compound the film's fundamental tragedy.

A second expensive white convertible features in Ralph Ellison's extraordinary short story "Cadillac Flambé."[25] There, arguments which remain mute and implicit in Perry Henzell's Jamaican images get spelled out explicitly and to dramatic effect. The story concerns the destruction by fire of a white Cadillac by its owner, Lee Willie Minifees, a disenchanted jazzman who has become unhappy with the meaning of his passionate attachment to his sleek, shiny car. The angry musician decides to sacrifice his well-appointed vehicle in a spectacular act of political theatre and metaphysical treachery, after he discovers that it may be a fetter on his freedom rather than a means to demonstrate his precious autonomy to the world.

He learns that the automobile has been described as a "coon cage" by a prominent senator and decides to stage the drama of immolation on the politician's estate as an act of defiance and revenge. The tableau of destruction alters the value that the senator has invested in an object which he regards as being tainted by its association with blackness.

Lee Willie responds to the politician's diagnosis of the pathological patterns of consumption found among American Negroes with a gesture of flamboyant renunciation which manages to be both absurd and pointed. He senses that his consumer appetites amount to a form of confinement and explains in detail that he and his kind should renounce their love of the things they have acquired as substitutes for their long-promised liberty. This scenario provides Ellison with an opportunity to explore the tension between consumerism and citizenship among African Americans, as well as to point to the gap between automotive freedom and freedom's other possible varieties.

Ellison describes the politician, Senator Sunraider, as a modern thinker who combines an interest in race with mastery of the "new political technology." Throughout the proceedings, an "innocent" narrator struggles to interpret the unfolding events at a distance, through his bird-watching binoculars. The musician wears a white suit. The car has white-walled tyres and a cream leather interior. The wood alcohol and petrol that fuel Lee Willie's sacrificial fire are also described as white.

As one might expect from Ellison, this auto-da-fé is not ideologically cast or politically doctrinaire. He seeks no resolution of the tensions he has conjured up, striving instead to air the problems produced by the moral and metaphysical aporia that is symbolised by the two racialised actors who supply margins for the page upon which the history of black America's consumer behaviour and its relationship to U.S. democracy will be recorded. The bass player certainly loves his beautiful car and thought not only that owning and driving it demonstrated his freedom but that those experiences comprised the substance of freedom itself. The dilemma Ellison presents involves a clear distinction between the traditional means of self making—the technology of the free black self— and the forms of freedom involved in consuming objects which, though you have chosen them for yourself, effectively come to dominate you. Ellison was no Marxist, but the rumbling approach of a theory of alienation should be obvious: "'But I paid for it, it's mine, I own it . . .' I said. 'Oh no, Lee Willie,' the voice said, 'what you mean is that it owns *you*. That's why you're in the cage. Admit it, daddy, you have been named.'"[26]

From his Californian eyrie, Adorno counterpointed this observation with some equally difficult insights into the deep cultural processes that connect driving, freedom, and the compromised democracy of the United States.[27] As a refugee from Nazi Germany, where cheap cars and high speed limits had become an integral part of the freedoms afforded by the Third Reich's militarised civic order,[28] he may have been nostalgic for earlier phases of "automobilism"—the days when motor vehicles were not allowed to exceed four miles an hour on public highways and were required to follow a guard with a red flag. Watching the United

States through the distorted lenses of an exile, he had noticed the nor-
mative place of walking start to fade and the liberal era that could be
defined by the rhythm of the bourgeois promenade displaced by the altogether different tempo supplied largely by wholesale resort to the private car. Struggling with these difficult problems in the period before
joggers became a familiar sight in U.S. cities and their suburbs, Adorno
also noted some of the ways in which the disturbance created by running in the street could bear witness not only to the past, primal terrors
of our species but to the continuing vulnerability of frail humanity in
harsh urban environments which had become inhospitable to the extent that walking had died out there. Any residual terror could be effectively mastered by "deflecting it from one's own body and at the same
time effortlessly surpassing it" in the cults of speed and sport that have
done so much to define our own anxious time. In turn, this seems to
suggest that the destructive automobile and its undoubted pleasures
should be understood in a historical setting shaped by the flight, restlessness, and mobility that characterised American society in its transition to mass automotivity and the new conceptions of speed and space
that derived from it.

All these enigmatic observations can be employed to reflect upon the
particular responses of African Americans to automotivity. Their histories of racial terror, brutal confinement, and coerced labour must have
given them additional receptivity to the pleasures of auto-autonomy as a
means of escape, transcendence, and, perhaps fleetingly, also of resistance.

I should probably repeat that this heuristic consideration of automotivity within the wider framework of America's racial politics is not a
means to present U.S. blacks as special dupes of consumerism. Instead,
it is intended to raise the provocative possibility—first suggested eight
decades ago by the early research on their spending habits—that a distinctive history of propertylessness and material deprivation may have
inclined African Americans towards a disproportionate investment in

particular forms of property that are publicly visible and in the status that corresponds to them. It has also contributed to a problematic tendency to conceive culture itself as a form of property which is held as compensation for low status and heavily restricted access to both rights and wealth.

Ellison and the others help us to appreciate the automobile in its proper historical and sociological position: at the very centre of America's complex negotiations with its own absurd racial codings. African American car cultures can certainly signify that the official scripts of respectable domesticity and deferred gratification have been rejected. At the same time, they can also suggest that those dreams have already been surpassed—overtaken—by more powerful and reckless desires which can be examined through the predisposition to what the marketing literature calls "status purchasing." There can be no doubt that cars lie at the heart of the informal, individual acts of symbolic redress with which some U.S. blacks have salved the chronic injuries of racialised hierarchy. We need to be able to understand the weak and fading patterns of resistance or struggle that are being articulated in that market, in that moral economy. However, it would also be wrong to overlook the possibility that the same flamboyant gestures of disavowal from the informal regulations of the colour-coded mainstream are being combined with other factors. A lingering negativity betrays black citizens' desire to join in the carnival of American plenitude as full participants in ways that racism used to deny. This may even be the muffled historical engine of the excessive "bling bling" style which has lately been so prominent within African American popular culture. Accommodation with and subordination to power are accomplished by means of another, related yearning. It is an unsubversive will to triumph in the game of consumerism and thereby to make consumer citizenship and brand identities eclipse the merely political forms of belonging promoted by governmental institutions. In securing that triumph for capitalism, the totemic, sublime power of the motor car demands fresh consideration

of the ways in which both the resistance and the resignation of black political interests are to be understood and evaluated.

Yet this is not just an argument about the limitations of consumer
freedom. It is a plea to consider the specific forms of freedom promoted
and withheld where car culture has shaped a racialised and segregated
polity. The outcome represents a diminution of citizenship, and it is associated with a privatisation that confiscates the possibility of collective
experience, synchronised suffering, and acting in concert. In these circumstances, the automobile becomes the instrument of segregation and
privatisation, not an aid to their overcoming.

This critical standpoint provides a gateway into a more motivated political history of car cultures than is currently at hand. It asks, for example, whether a more hostile discussion of automobiles and their
social and psychological consequences might help us to clarify and perhaps rethink the very nature of black political formations at this pivotal,
postcolonial stage in their planetary development. This is not only because a critical assessment of cars and car culture can yield productive
questions about the notions of progress, development, growth, wealth,
and prosperity and their relation to unchallenged and apparently invul-
nerable industrial, postindustrial, and commercial capitalisms. It bears
repeating that the current wars in Afghanistan and Mesopotamia involve a geo-politics of energy, as well as the imperial interests of the
United States. Both of these factors have complex relationships to the
changing character of U.S. racial hierarchy. Both represent a contemporary test of the old "closing ranks" argument first articulated by Du
Bois in response to the First World War, which he believed could bring
African American citizenship alive in proportion to the willingness of
his countrymen to sacrifice their lives for their nation on the battlefield.[29] Today, it may be better to see their military service as the terminal point of a double consciousness that has been resolved not as he
imagined it would be, into a higher and better self which coincided with
the lofty imperatives of world citizenship, but into the different mood

set by the restless demands of insatiable consumers in the "Rich Dad, Poor Dad" generation.

Where cars were available only in limited quantities and remained a luxury item—a big, noisy, polluting badge of relative prosperity—they were insufficient to orchestrate a car culture or animate the antisocial nature of car-based civilisation. Once ownership became affordable and widespread, however, they enveloped social and economic relations and, in the process, undermined the very idea of public good. The United States reached the statistical level of one car per household during the 1920s. Mass automobility posed fundamental problems of social solidarity and political connection even among minority populations where levels of ownership were lowest. This remains an especially acute danger for black communities seeking to resist local confinement in the postindustrial ghetto[30] and searching for new ways of becoming present to one another amidst the techno-cultural ferment of the information age.

In many parts of the world, the automobile and attitudes toward it provided further tests of consumer capitalism and its power to depoliticise, disorient, and mystify. Analysis of car use can illuminate the quiet enforcement of racially—and therefore economically—segregated space that is a growing feature of metropolitan life in many overdeveloped countries. Automobility also helps to show up the deepening lines of class division found in dispersed racial communities that are now anything but spontaneously solid, homogenous, or unified.[31]

Tracking changing attitudes towards the car, through good and bad times, recession and expansion, resurgence and defeat, can also be instructive. For much of the twentieth century, the private automobile, and the social order it supported, constituted something like an index of hegemony. In the United States, the inadequacies of public transport confirmed and cemented the appeal of radically individualistic solutions and communicated the general defeat of the idea of public or common good.

Watching the regressive modernisation of Britain with growing alarm, a weary-sounding Raymond Williams was among the first commentators to grasp the significance of this "mobile privatisation" for social relations in the "old industrial countries." The increased privatisation of life and its fragmentation into active, small-family units was being combined with an unprecedented degree of mobility. Williams decided to use the image of modern car traffic to capture the deadly ambiguities in this combination, which, he felt, characterised the whole unsettling experience of being in a consumer society:

> Looked at from right outside, the traffic flows and their regulation are clearly a social order of a determined kind, yet what is experienced inside them—in the conditioned atmosphere and internal music of this windowed shell—is movement, choice of direction, the pursuit of self-determined private purposes. All the other shells are moving, in comparable ways but for their own different private ends. They are not so much other people, in any full sense, but other units that signal and are signaled to, so that private mobilities can proceed safely and relatively unhindered. And if all this is seen from the outside as in deep ways determined, or in some sweeping glance as de-humanised, that is not at all how it feels inside the shell, with people you want to be with going where you want to go.[32]

I want to go further than Williams and to suggest that a historical consideration of the car's totemic power can provide analytical tools with which to illuminate neglected aspects of the twentieth century's black freedom struggles and of their complex relationship to the racially stratified societies from which they sprang. These were social movements animated by people who had very good reasons to fear the constraints involved in being tied to one place. That anxiety may well have inclined them towards the pleasures of speed, autonomy, and privatised transport, quite apart from their attraction to the automobile as a pro-vocative emblem for the wealth and status they desired but were so often denied. Their conspicuous enthusiasm for the private car and their sub-sequent difficulties in seeing beyond its windscreen reveal how those movements and their conceptions of freedom have been transformed, compromised, distracted, and diverted. Today, the decay of those for-mations has helped to deliver us to the historic point where blackness can easily become less an index of hurt, resistance, or solidarity in the face of persistent and systematic inequality, than one more faintly ex-otic lifestyle "option" conferred by the multicultural alchemy of heavily branded commodities and the presealed, "ethnic" identities that ap-parently match them in a world where globalisation is, to all intents and purposes, a process of (North)Americanisation.[33]

From this perspective, solidarity ends and danger arises when free-dom entails little more than winning a long-denied opportunity to shop on the same terms as other, more privileged citizens further up the wob-bly ladder of racial hierarchy and economic advantage. In other words, it would appear that a significant measure of respect and recognition capable of mediating or reversing the effects of subordination can now simply be bought, or, if not, at least simulated with the help of the right range of props. The desired social effects are conferred on purchasers by objects that they own, display, or manipulate.

In their own eyes, and perhaps also in the eyes of others, these sub-jected people become different in the light of their heavily branded vis-ibility. Beyond any functionality, any use value, and all metaphysics of utility,[34] these users—who may have leased, borrowed, or even stolen the goods to which they publicly demonstrate their access—have parked themselves between two poles where symbolic value can be negotiated. We can call the first of these locations *shoppers' rebellion*. There, the offi-cial value given to these prizes by a world of work and wages is sup-posedly altered, or at least ironically commented upon, in a counter-axiology which may become quite elaborate. The second pole, *shoppers' resignation,* is defined most obviously by the mood of individuals who want to answer the sour impact of racism on their lives by buying in rather than dropping out. They accept prestigious objects as a means to seem wealthier, prouder, and thus more respectable, more worthy of recognition. Both of these responses produce high-risk strategies when the link between commodities and identities is accepted. Luxury and other heavily branded goods have been deliberately invested with seasonal fluctuations. Their details evolve rapidly and restlessly. The forms of attention required in order to track those changes at high tempo can release violent envy and compound the petty hatreds of a steeply segregated world in which the interplay of material privilege and racial hierarchy is necessarily complex.

David Nye, the insightful historian of energy, has pinpointed some of the tragic consequences that can follow when this transient yet intimate bond is carried over into the world of automotivity: "To the extent that the buyer invested personal meaning in a car, its obsolescence underlined how unstable the sense of identity can be when underwritten by consumption."[35] With that alarming possibility in mind, it should be easier to see that the car and car worship distill all the moral and political difficulties of consumerism into the purest and most potent forms.

If that association between identity and object sounds perilous, some of the more liberatory aspects of twentieth-century African American car use should also be acknowledged. An interesting example is bell hooks's striking memoir of her Jim Crow childhood. As the civil rights movement reached her small hometown in rural Kentucky, the special freedom that Raymond Williams identified—namely, the ability to travel fast and stylishly with people of one's own choosing—became invested with a strong democratic and counter-cultural charge. That combination of qualities brought the transitional phase of high school desegregation to vivid life:

> We are looking for ourselves beyond the sign of race. Nature
> is the only place we can go where race leaves us. We can ride

this car way out. . . . At first I am not sure I want to cross the
tracks to make nice with a white girl but the smell of the car
seduces me. Its leather seats, the real wood on the dashboard,
the shiny metal so clear it's like glass—like a mirror it dares to
move past race to take to the road and find ourselves—find the
secret places within where there is no such thing as race.[36]

The antiracist dimension of this history of transgressive freedom-
seeking needs to be noted, but that minor victory was dearly bought. It
arrived at the cost of a triumph for the most mainstream pleasures of car
culture. Should the powerful sense of liberation be judged secondary to
the destructive and corrosive consequences of automotivity and privatised motorisation? Was this a small victory over segregation or its refinement?

Part of the explanation for the disturbing combination of consumer
freedom with elective confinement lies in the fact that in spite of their
sufferings, or perhaps because of them, African Americans were enthusiastic about the automobile revolution almost from its inception.[37] In
other words, they were alert to the pleasures and opportunities afforded
them by automotivity for some time before the manufacturers began to
target them as a distinctive group of buyers.

The Poetics of Transit

As the color-line century progressed, North America's black freedom
movements engaged what can be called the poetics of transit. The journeys of ex-slaves and their latter-day descendants to the promised land
without racial hierarchy were always going to be made on foot or, where
that was not practicable, undertaken by freedom train and desegregated
bus. "People get ready, there's a train a comin'" and "Stop That Train"
were the respective cries of Curtis Mayfield and Peter Tosh. Sam Cooke's
baby arrived back by train. James Brown's J.B.'s traveled by monorail,
not superfly limousine. All those busy locomotives were on the over-

ground railroad: a noisy, visible, and powerful symbol that inverted—conjured with—the colonial potency of the industrial technologies to which white supremacy and its signature unfreedoms were coupled. Houston A. Baker Jr. brilliantly unraveled some of the interpretive tangles presented by those "traditional" railroad tracks, train whistles, and crossing points and the world of coerced labour from which they stemmed.[38] The courageous, volkish preparedness to be even just a "headlight on a northbound train" in order to escape from the terroristic, disabling world of Jim Crow can be understood best where his important insights have been absorbed, but the place of automotive transportation in the same semantic and mimetic fields has been seldom approached with comparable rigor and clarity.

W. T. Lhamon Jr.'s acute reading of Chuck Berry's "motorvatin'" songs comes closest to showing where that missing link might be located. Lhamon is particularly insightful when it comes to the song "Maybellene," an epic car chase narrative from 1955 that Berry had adapted into the idiom of rock and roll from an earlier country song by Bob Wills; and "Promised Land," a later, more portentously poetic telling of cross-country travel which represents a complex act of conjuring with the topography and transit-culture of the freedom rides.

Lhamon rightly places the Berry of songs like "You Can't Catch Me" in the lineage of the minstrel show, but the new postwar era was marked by an accelerated insubordination. The change was easiest to behold in black America's altered relationship with the automobile and the pleasures of driving. The narrator pursuing Maybellene in her expensive Cadillac was behind the wheel of a cheaper, more proletarian Ford. Reflecting on the song's crafty deployment of sex and Berry's artful switching between descriptions of the fast, elusive woman and her powerful vehicle, Lhamon concludes: "A man who has overcome his victimization by chasing down the fanciest Cadillac on a rainy road, intuitively drawn on the language and riffs of his folkways, intertwined them with that twang and rhythm of his neighbors' counter tradition, and snuck his resulting anthem of pride past all the natural and cultural roadblocks—what might such a sly agent do with straying Maybellene at their peak moment?"[39]

Setting aside the impact of Berry's critical commentary on automobile salesmen in "No Money Down" (1956), his most successful 1960s tune, "No Particular Place To Go" (1964), suggests that Lhamon's astute question may also be missing the most important point. Ten years after "Maybellene" had been banned from BBC airplay because of its references to commercial products, the culture of the automobile which Berry had previously hitched to his ulterior purposes had undermined the significance of all arrivals, destinations, and outcomes. Berry's song "Nadine" starts on a city bus and ends in a taxi: a transformation which underscores how the point had changed. Berry's speedy protagonists were now unlikely to *do* anything, because by this time just being in the car, using its safety belts or steering it (if only around the parking lot), had become ends in themselves rather than means. The new freedom affirmed so cryptically in Berry's subtly subversive lyrics and so openly in his dancing on stage was most powerfully communicated by the absence of any approved or official end to that fateful encounter on the highway. This novel freedom began and terminated with the declaration that, in spite of the narrative momentum he brought to the form, there was no particular place to go precisely because the car was now a topos of its own.

Berry's map of the hazards involved in these unprecedented automotive journeys was misleading only where it suggested an antagonistic relationship between the country and the city. The image of the roadblock, which he shared with Bob Marley among others, compressed all the existential perils of driving while black. Cars belonged first to the city, not the woods. Yet all the environments that they entered and changed were reconstituted around their devastating presence.

Automobiles transformed the life of black communities everywhere and would help to produce the polar opposition of ghetto and suburb.

Inside the former, they fostered a new conception of the street as a place of danger and violence rather than of community, creativity, and mutuality.[40] Even those achievements were only a fraction of the motor car's revolutionary significance. Today, its neglected history still helps to articulate important interpretive and political lessons. It obliges us to update our understanding of culture itself in order to accommodate mobility and speed and their transformation of space, as well as to acknowledge the entrenched divisions between public and private that ludic technologies promoted and invested with new meaning once the private could traverse the public with pleasure and with ease.

Along this route, we are also required to adjust the way we understand commodities. These automobiles were products, but we have already seen that they could also be conspicuously productive. Their shiny authority and their antisocial prestige alike entailed something more than just the endpoint of industrial capital's mystified economic circuits. It bears repeating: they were the *ur*-commodity, and as such they help to periodise capitalism as it moves into and leaves its industrial phase. They also politicise and moralise everyday life in unprecedented configurations. In doing so, the curved, reflexive surfaces they provide can show us our distorted selves. Their hold over us reveals how particular objects and technologies can become, in effect, active, dynamic social forces in the material cultures of everyday life. Their power compels acknowledgement of the conditions under which technological resources can acquire the characteristics of historical agents and social actors.

Cars fudge any residual distinctions between material and semiotic, base and superstructure, by defying the assumed fixity which gave that powerful spatial metaphor its initial analytic grip. Automotive culture therefore provides a primary challenge to all aspiring theories of consumption and postmodernity. Analyzing it demands that we modify our understanding of consumer society and its workings, so that our analysis can encompass the alienated but nonetheless popular pleasures of auto-freedom (mobility, power, and speed) while appreciating their conspicuous interpersonal, civic, environmental, and geo-political costs.[41]

Wherever car culture reshaped society, even where consumerism was not the dominant economic mode, that triumph placed technology and power squarely in the middle of ordinary life, which was transformed by the ways that cars redefined movement and prosthetically extended sensory experience. We need to be able to examine the workings of this ordinary potency within power's wider circuitry: governmental, metropolitan, ecological, and of course economic. The history of black communities and automotivity can help to accomplish all these tasks. However, the privatisation of mobility and experience associated with these large historical changes is difficult to interpret solely under the sign of racial difference. The moment of liberation that was typified in bell hooks's journeying and promised in Lee Willie Minifees' original, untainted love for his expensive Cadillac should not be exaggerated, but neither can it be ignored. It would be too simple if the car became nothing more than a vehicle for the compromise and accommodation of tamed black interests to a resurgent consumer capitalism, freshly unconfined by the Cold War.

In January 2008, the California-based Strategic Vision consultancy announced the results of extensive research into the racial aspects of the automobile market.[42] Using what they termed a "value-centered method," they set out to narrate how the emotional and psychological characteristics of different racial groups were expressed in their likely choice of motor vehicle. This research had been done to assist manufacturers and sellers in building brand equity and loyalty while catering to the specific needs of these different groups. Their press release is worth quoting at length:

> Differences that clearly stand out with African Americans are greater desires for success and the ability to show it. African Americans are much more likely to advocate vehicles that ex-

press their individuality and success to family and friends.
Latinos have a greater concern for the impact on the environment while also exhibiting a greater desire to experience exhilarating driving and performance than others. Asian Americans have stronger demands for a balanced, complete vehicle
performance and style that matches their lives.

These race-specific seductions aside, the U.S. highways produced an
artificial space where all the people driving these dangerous machines
could encounter one another as formal equals, even if the necessary
privacy of their individual transit experiences contributed to the way
that they lived out their widening social separation. The highway produced a uniquely powerful sense of the peculiar historical and political
logic of "separate but equal."

During the interwar years the Swedish sociologist Gunnar Myrdal, in
his landmark study *An American Dilemma,* had noted a significant relationship between car use and racial equality. Yet the pattern evident in
the market for consumer goods since the 1940s suggests that the acquisition of new things could not be relied upon to promote cultural or experiential convergence between black and white. The Negro was judged,
relative to the white, as a bad consumer whose rational purchasing and
aspirations were distorted by cultural factors. More than that, having
the same stuff did not inevitably promote a sense of kinship or foster
forms of reciprocal human recognition against the stern force of racial
absolutes. There has been a tendency to develop parallel or niche markets and to address diverse groups of consumers in their own languages
or idioms, if not more directly through their ethnic identities. This arrangement also lent that phrase "separate but equal" greater plausibility
and made ethnic and racial particularities into a container for communities stratified by wealth. Once Negroes could buy cars, hold drivers'
licenses, and obtain auto insurance, car culture and the unwholesome
desires it kindled seem to have become key components in what kept

the wealthier and more privileged of them squarely in the middle of the road. The aspirations of their poorer racial siblings were channeled towards the goal of changing their abject status by acquiring objects rather than rights.

These problems have intensified in contemporary societies where one is socially appraised by what one owns or uses, and where the boundaries of relative deprivation have been redrawn by fantasies of celebrity, rising personal debt, inflated expectations, and ignorance of what the normal economic rewards of a working life actually add up to.[43]

The reconfiguration of consumer culture into plural, nominally multicultural forms needs a detailed history, but that cannot be provided here. Suffice to say that it has been intertwined with the battles to win civil rights and recognition, that it has been a potent and enduring source of confusion with regard to the combination of race and class hierarchies, and that it has contributed to the reproduction of strongly racialised conceptions of gender, identity, and sexuality.

Global Immanence as Americanisation

Though Europeans had invented the petrol-powered car, it rapidly became an overwhelmingly American technology.[44] The initial European dominance of car production was over by 1904, and the quality of U.S. cars improved rapidly. In what was an essentially urban market, Americans were soon far more likely to own cars than their European counterparts. As the twentieth century progressed, cars emerged as a potent presence in the newly imperial nation's fantasies of metropolitan order, commerce, and reform. The automobile would improve public health and end the urban pollution problems that were being caused by horses.[45] David Nye reminds us that for much of the twentieth century, automobile production was the very "engine of the American economy, stimulating a wide range of subsidiary industries and suppliers."[46]

It bears emphasis that because cars were a U.S. phenomenon, they were comprehensively entangled in that fractured nation's politics of racial hierarchy. Initially, automobiles had been exclusively presented to white consumers. Some companies expressly stipulated that their machines should not be sold even to those few blacks who could afford them. For African American populations seeking ways out of the lingering shadows of slavery, owning and using automobiles supplied one significant means to measure the distance traveled towards political freedoms and public respect. Employed in this spirit, cars seem to have conferred or rather suggested dimensions of citizenship and status that were blocked by formal politics and violently inhibited by informal social codes.

Later, the same freedom-seeking people would be confined to the disabling options represented by rural poverty on one side and inner-city immiseration on the other. Here again, the car provided handy solutions to the eco-political problems it had occasioned and multiplied. Many African Americans were actively disadvantaged by social and economic changes which made the car into an absolute necessity if employment was to be sought and maintained. The memoir by bell hooks suggested a counter-narrative to this story of marginalisation; but when the Jim Crow system of segregation was eventually broken, it would be the same motor car that provided both blacks and whites with tacit, complementary solutions to the discomforts of traveling in close proximity with each other. For blacks, driving themselves could be part of their belated liberation from their U.S. apartheid, while for whites, the same tactic supplied a legitimate means of perpetuating and indeed compounding segregation in the new forms created by essentially privatised transport between suburban dwellings in racially homogenous neighbourhoods and distant employment opportunities. White flight from urban centres was not just accomplished by means of the automobile—it was premised on it.

Needless to say, once they were officially allowed to do so, U.S. blacks bought cars at least as readily as their economic circumstances permitted. Indeed, because their public display of wealth had been restricted, cars acquired an additional significance in their complex counter-cultures as signs of insubordination, progress, and compensatory prestige.

Reconstructing the history of that moral economy and what we can call its resistance/resignation behaviours takes us all the way back to the usefully monumental figure of the famous boxer Jack Johnson. He was heavyweight champion of the world in bold and sometimes reckless defiance of the masculinist codes of white supremacy during the first years of the color-line century. His well-proportioned ghost remains a significant residual presence even in the different mediascapes adumbrated on the one hand by Michael Jordan's global stardom and on the other by Ice Cube's ironic reworking of the same themes in the Hollywood comedy *Are We There Yet?* In Cube's case, the postmodern index of black masculinity becomes the difficult task of stepfathering disrespectful, car-destroying black children rather than the illegal squiring of car-appreciating white womanhood across state lines.[47]

Johnson's place in the bitter political conflicts over manliness, masculinity, and "race" that greeted the century of the color line has been considered at length by other writers.[48] Their accounts have not usually been engaged by his inauguration of distinctive patterns in the way that automobiles were understood and articulated within and sometimes against U.S. racial rules. Johnson's manliness and his ambiguous stardom were expressed in and through his command of cars. His driving drew hostility, harassment, and an introjected, covetous admiration from the police wherever he went. This was partly a reaction to the presence of white women in Johnson's cars, but it should also be recognised as involving responses to those cars themselves and to the uncomfortable idea of a black man at the wheel of a speeding vehicle. We miss the enduring significance of Johnson's exemplary life if we emphasise one of these factors at the expense of the others. Though he was among the first African Americans to fall foul of the law for the informal crime of

"driving while black," Johnson's well-known love of cars and speed entered into his mythification at different points far removed from the
contested space of the public thoroughfare.

In October 1910, at the height of his visibility, Johnson challenged
the fastest drivers of the day to a race in which the victor could claim
$5,000 of his money. The professional racer Barney Oldfield responded
enthusiastically to the prospect of a public contest that would inevitably
reflect upon the respective capacities of their racial groups in the emergent worlds of motor-sport and celebrity sportsmen. The American Automobile Association threatened to bar Oldfield from their organisation
if he took part in this unwelcome event, which was staged in front of
some 5,000 spectators and a film crew at Sheepshead Bay on Coney Island. Johnson, driving a bright red, 90-horsepower Thompson Flyer,
was comprehensively defeated by his opponent, who took the wheel of a
60-horsepower Knox.[49] The *New York Sun* greeted Oldfield's victory with
the famous headline, "White Race Saved."[50]

It is telling that Johnson, an aristocrat of the body who encapsulated
the twentieth-century Negro's supposedly rapturous relationship with
physicality, failed to triumph in this domain, where mental attributes
rather than natural reflexes were apparently decisive. The car provided
an important new medium for the evaluation of those racialised qualities. The inferiority of the "inferior" races could now be communicated
through the idea that they were poorer drivers.

Cars and motor sport were both commodities produced by the very
same exploitative interests that played such an important role in building the racial division of labour which would characterise America's industrial capitalism as it moved to articulate production and consumption[51] in a Fordist shape. A critical history of car culture might be useful
in a bid to restore missing elements of black America's collective political memory with regard to the long transition between slavery and freedom. One small element of this would be precious knowledge of the

complex connections between black freedom struggles and organised working-class interests that were found in Ford's corporate headquarters. In Detroit, Malcolm X would later be just one more worker on the assembly line producing Ford trucks. The ready racialisation of Fordism by its footsoldiers and its architects raises another issue—namely, the racially divided factory production which also needs to be placed in relation to the history of slavery if its links with the world of waged labour are to be properly understood.[52]

Nobody can quarrel with the suggestion that Henry Ford was a white supremacist, even if his unqualified contempt for the Negro was sometimes articulated in paternalistic form. His anti-Semitism had been spelled out at an early stage in his tract *The International Jew: The World's Foremost Problem*, which had brought his ideas and achievements to Hitler's admiring attention. There is no need to overinterpret the well-documented mutual admiration of the two men. In *Mein Kampf*, Hitler praised Ford's ability to remain independent against the pressures of international Jewry, and Ford accepted the Grand Cross of the German Eagle from the Nazi government in 1938. This sort of information—like the news that Ford Werke, the German division of the Ford Company, gave Hitler a 35,000-Reichsmark birthday present in 1939 and had deployed the unfree labour of French, Russians, Ukrainians, and Belgians even before the Nazis placed its plant in "trusteeship"—should complicate our understanding of the relationship between Fordism and Fascism. At both ends of that historic chain, the car and automotive freedoms were bound to the private, modern leisure promoted by authoritarian and race-friendly regimes: one corporate, the other governmental.[53]

We've already encountered Chuck Berry's playful, insubordinate motorvatin' as one example of how the forms of liberation and autonomy promoted by cars could be impossible to confine in a segregated world that was becoming more affluent. Berry's teen-oriented tales were components of a sly African American tradition in which automobiles were serenaded and savoured in accordance with an aesthetic approach that valued movement over fixity and sometimes prized public style over private comfort and security. Motor vehicles could be public ciphers of celebrity; and as Ellison showed, musicians and entertainers in particular appreciated the powerful poetic possibilities that flashy, fast, and fancy cars created. The paeans these artists offered to their own transportation, to private car travel, to speed, and even to the *idea* of the car itself might be used today to construct a shadow history of the shifting appeal of consumer culture to those marginal populations who had not initially been targeted by manufacturers but for whom the dreamworld of American consumer culture held the most potent appeal, precisely because of their exclusion from its heavily fortified land of promise.

   We should recall that the very first verses of that founding text of twentieth-century African American folklore, the toast "Staggolee," refer to the eponymous hero's "'28 Ford."[54] Eight years later, Robert Johnson's first popular recording, "Terraplane Blues," was one of the first race records to link the motor car to the female body and driving to sex. Johnson's promises to check the oil, flash the lights, and get under the hood open up a curious path through the remainder of the twentieth century. That route proceeds from Berry to R. Kelly, whose "You Remind Me of Something" is a song that plumbs the depths of estrangement by suggesting that the love of objects, in this case a jeep, now provides a strange template from which the blank dimensions of troubled interpersonal desire are to be shaped. This carborne journey through the psycho-sexual backwoods of consumer society proceeds by a circuitous route. Albert King's weary complaints against the neo-slave labour that claimed him on the Cadillac assembly line are only partially redeemed by K. C. Douglas' classic appreciation of the Mercury—a recording memorable for the fact that, like Berry's, it spanned the adjacent but often antagonistic musical worlds of blues and country. On this pilgrimage to the corporate headquarters of *DUB* magazine in California, we overtake Sam Cooke and Miles Davis in their Ferraris and pass Aretha in her pink Cadillac (just like the one Elvis had bought in 1955). Think for a moment about the different "ethnic" options those brand choices might be used to represent. We press on through Jimi Hendrix's cross-town traffic, which articulates more echoes of slavery and presents the woman not as a car herself but as an obstacle blocking the male driver's unobstructed access to the city (the song was annexed to provide the soundtrack for a Volkswagen advertisement). Further on up this road, we encounter Prince's little red Corvette and the New Power Generation's "Deuce and a Quarter" (a shocking hymn of appreciation to that ghetto chariot, the Buick Electra 225). We are delivered finally to the terminal point provided some sixty years beyond "Terraplane Blues" by TLC's global hit "No Scrubs," in which the irremediable uselessness of the unworthy black man in question was conveyed and confirmed by the fact that he had no car of his own and had been spotted "hanging out of the passenger side of his best friend's ride."

It is not only, as the example drawn from Jack Johnson suggested, that car culture provides an important means to comprehend the techno-cultural dynamics of the black masculinity with which it was entangled from such an early point. I am certain, too, that an assessment of the impact of car culture can also contribute something distinctive to our understanding of the checkered history of black political activity.

The distinctive spatial arrangements involved in de facto and de jure forms of racial segregation no longer correspond to a similar mode of absolute cultural separation. An innocent event like the Motown Corporation's 1975 transcoding of the popular teens-and-cars movie *American Graffiti* into a free-standing, black, alternative version entitled *Cooley High* can be used—like the company's reworking of *The Wizard of Oz* for African American children, from the same pivotal period—to mark the emergence of more extensive operations in the fields of corporate multiculture, race branding, and ethnic "cluster marketing." Racialised products were tailored and targeted with precision at the groupings for whom they were most significant—that is, at the racial constituencies to which they were imagined to belong. The mechanisms of consumer culture were fragmented or, more politely, pluralised along the old lines of "race" and ethnicity. You got your version of the culture, and we got ours. Corporate multiculturalism has made that commercial landscape substantially more complicated.

Du Bois had said long ago that the motor car was a means to promote and distinguish the social and economic particularity of the black middle class. A much more elaborate car culture may now have become a way of foreclosing the possibility of any substantive connections between the privileged caste of U.S. blacks and other, less fortunate groups, both inside their own society and among the "third world" folk who live within the veil of scarcity defined, if they are lucky, by the alternative transit technology of the bicycle.

This angle of analysis foregrounds questions of race, class, and status. It interests me because I am acutely aware that thirty-plus years ago a radical, social ecology, pronounced from inside the core of black vernacular culture, cautiously identified the automobile among the most destructive technological innovations to have been produced on this planet. That critical stance was not alien to the dissenting articulation of black political interests by disenchanted, cosmopolitan African Americans.[55] The moral authority of that largely forgotten oppositional legacy must be considered again as a political resource for the future, not least because of the present need to develop responses to climate change.

That critique of consumerism, waste, and the contempt for nature is associated with a special phase in the life of soul and of rhythm and blues. It is infused with the shamanic authority of its key architects: Curtis Mayfield and Marvin Gaye. Today their work still raises alternative possibilities and suggests that, even though it may be hard to detect, there is, dormant in the same black idioms, a hostility to car culture which might once again provide vivid ways to make the disquieting perspective of a vernacular, "green" anticapitalism intelligible, especially among those who do not want to live in a warfare state oriented by the imperial pursuit of fossil fuel in distant lands. Though currently muted, that tradition of reflecting on the wrongs and woes of consumer society has wellsprings in the economic processes that saw black people themselves become commodities for sale on translocal markets. It has also been linked to a strong sense of political kinship between the African American nation and the world's colonised peoples, particularly in Africa. If those honest pleas to "downshift" could somehow be revived, they might be able to bring uncomfortable but unavoidable political and moral choices home to a new generation which has been entirely habituated to the car and its pleasures and which, as a result, finds alternatives to the cage of consumer capitalism exceedingly difficult if not impossible to imagine.

I do not want to be misunderstood. The historical role that car dealership and car loans have played in the development of autonomous economic activity and entrepreneurship among black Americans should not be lightly scorned. But it stands in stark opposition to the altogether different tone established by the less materialistic sentiments elaborated, for example, in William DeVaughn's classic song "Be Thankful for What You Got." This was a multimillion-selling, mid-Seventies recording that remains memorable for DeVaughn's righteous repudiation of car culture and its increasingly powerful claims on the racialised ontologies of the ghetto's desperate and immiserated inhabitants. It probably helped that DeVaughn, a guitar-playing Jehovah's Witness from Washington, D.C., cut his car-skeptical anthem in Philadelphia's Sigma Sound Studios. The TSOP house band were at the peak of their prodigious creative capacities, and their sinuous playing has sometimes helped to turn his pious attack on car consciousness into something of a driver's anthem. Nonetheless, the resulting record, with its memorable chorus of "Diamond in the back, sun-roof top, / Digging the scene with a gangsta lean," caught the historical energy of that transitional moment so comprehensively that it drew an interplanetary acknowledgement from George Clinton's Mothership and lives on today in a legacy of samples and cover versions—notably by Bristol's Massive Attack. DeVaughn's tune remains memorable for its disquieting opening lines, which offer eloquent testimony to what is now too often a heretical possibility—namely that "you may not have a car at all." He begins gently, not by posing the plight of the carless against the altogether different experience of the owner/driver but by acknowledging that an extravagantly fitted-out Cadillac would be out of reach of the people that he's primarily interested in speaking to. "You may not drive a great big Cadillac," he continues, but "remember, brothers and sisters, you can still stand tall."[56] DeVaughn's wholesome sentiment is a very long way from Missy Elliott's insistent, insinuating request to know "Beep beep, who got the keys to the Jeep?" a celebration of the experience of rolling with the ragtop down that counterposed the spirits of the Seventies and the Nineties.[57] Though Missy was alive to the symbolic dimensions of the SUV's value in her cityscape, that automobile was still an instrument which served a function she could control.

Seven years later, in the midst of a moral panic over the nihilistic ferment produced by the narco economy and the society of mass incarceration, 50 Cent's "Get Rich or Die Tryin'" (2003) offered another bulletin from the hood, where "they identify niggaz by they cars." His restless gangsta narrator explains that he "switch up whips to stay off the radar" and goes on to boast about being "in the Benz on Monday, the BM on Tuesday, Range on Wednesday, Thursday I'm in the hooptay, Porsche on Friday, I do things my way: Vipe or Vette, I tear up the highway." More disturbing than the scenes of violent excess that are celebrated is the glimpse that is provided not merely of the Negro as an object among other objects, but of the way that these objects interact with their alienated black owner/user, who displaces his subjectivity and agency into them so that they can accomplish things on his behalf. The track "Poor Little Rich" captures the same odd arrangement. Once again, the automobile supplies the dominant, recurrent point of reference in a dismal sequence in which the agency of the speaker has been displaced into a communicative work accomplished on his behalf by his own possessions. He imagines that these beautiful objects will speak eloquently while he remains stylishly mute: "my watch saying 'hi shorty we can be friends,' my whip saying 'quit playing bitch and get in,' my earring saying 'we can hit the mall together, shorty it's only right that we ball together.'" 50 Cent continues, "My chromes cost more than the crib ya momma raised ya in." The song's chorus explains the narrator's upward trajectory and symptomatically terminates in the conspicuous pleasures of mobile privatisation, which have clearly intensified in the interim: "I was a poor nigga, now I'm a rich nigga getting paper, now you can't tell me shit nigga. You can find me in the fo' dot six nigga. In the backseat fondling ya bitch nigga." Three years later the hip hop anthem "Chevy Ridin' High," by Dre (André Lyon) and Rick Ross, confirmed the destination of the journey that Robert Johnson had started decades earlier. Johnson had appreciatively compared his lover's body to an automobile, investing her human flesh with the hardness, sleekness, and style of a machine which he, as the mechanic, had the specialised knowledge to fix and maintain. The mood of the Black Power era was quite different. On their 1965 recording "A Woman's Got Soul," the Impressions had effectively overwritten that scheme with a heartfelt assertion that the love of a soulful woman was qualitatively different from interacting with any object. That intimate experience had a different public significance. Specifically, it was both more valuable and more important than a relationship with either cars or riches. The car emerged here not just as less desirable than a soulful woman. It was an object that put the possibility of a properly soulful relationship into psychological and historical perspective. With the car excluded from intersubjective drama, the authentic value of intimacy between soulful men and women could be discovered and savoured. "I don't need a Cadillac car or diamonds and such . . . And then I'm richer than the richest gold . . . If the woman's got soul."

Rick Ross signalled the imploded alienation that characterises twenty-first-century consumer culture by explaining that, even without actually driving his vehicle, the pleasure he derived from interacting with it was equal to the joys of sex itself. His car was preferable to a woman! "I got a V12, sweeter than a female / It feels like intercourse bucklin' the seatbelt."[58]

The End of Black Nationalism

Notwithstanding Suzanne E. Smith's arguments for a political and economic linkage between the Detroit car industry and the productive regime established in the earlier forms of African American popular culture pioneered by Berry Gordy's Motown hit factory,[59] it is very strange indeed that the economic strategies favoured by postmodern African American cultural nationalists should be quite so preoccupied with the riches to be won from dealing in automobiles and the signaling of wealth and status through the peculiar medium of automotive property. Cars, after all, are commodities produced by the very same exploitative corporations that played such an important role in constituting the racial division of labour in America's industrial capitalism.[60]

During the period of decolonisation and the era of Black Power that corresponded to it, the idea of liberation depended upon building a transnational bridge across the chasm of imperial exploitation and combined but uneven development. The idea that African American experience might be understood as a variety of internal colonialism was a notable result of this kind of connection. The contemporary naturalisation and celebration of car culture is a blunt sign that those valuable connections are becoming harder to secure. New possibilities for solidarity and translocal action are required now that corporate powers can routinely challenge and sometimes even eclipse governmental statecraft, acting with even less regard for the territory they exploit than any colonial administration would be able to do. The recent campaign against unsustainable car culture raised from within the heart of overdevelopment has been notably enriched by its connections to the pursuit of rights in areas of the developing world where oil companies and mineral extractors have held human life, the biosphere, and the commons in contempt. Opposition to the record of the oil conglomerate Shell in Nigeria provides some of the best recent examples here. Oblique connections of this type help to make the car and its cultures into a different kind of issue by opposing the family romance of national raciality to the intractable facts of global economic inequality. The longed-for continuities of a singular black identity are wrecked by the gulf that divides the southern realms of necessity from northern kingdoms, where scarcity, though hardly unknown, is not an essential precondition for social interaction.

After the occupation of Iraq, the oil-seeking, neo-imperial dynamic was delivered back home, transmitted deep into the tissue of the everyday. Thus, the car can help to delineate the basic political and economic divisions that distinguish globalisation, particularly those that would sunder the overdeveloped parts of the planet from the rest. Of course, from another angle, we should not ignore the deepening inequalities and persistent poverty that can be found inside the glittering fortifications of car-saturated, overdeveloped zones. Similarly, the widening gap between that world and the systematically underdeveloped spaces on the planet is not visible only in the patterning of transnational relations.

The postcolonial metropolis is host to a massive discrepancy in material conditions and life chances which is evident even when the groups involved dwell in close proximity. In many U.S. cities, this growing inequality can be understood as a local instance of our planet's north/south divisions. It constitutes acute local problems to which resolutely privatised transport—often, it would seem, in paramilitary vehicles—presents an attractive solution. The motor car has helped to disseminate and popularise the absolute social segregation that previously characterised the colonial city but which is now a widespread feature of the postcolonial metropolis, where security is at a premium and life chances increasingly correspond to locality.

Recognising what these social, spatial, and economic arrangements owe to the colonial past generates additional interpretive opportunities. We can, for example, observe the way taxi driving became race-coded service work and then ceased being so. We are able precisely to measure the developmental gaps between being a chauffeur, wanting a chauffeur, and having a chauffeur. The chauffeur, a servant who is intimately positioned between the car owner and the work of driving, was paradigmatic of the whole new world of casual and insecure work. The driven were being placed in a new position. Their partial removal from the world of risk was the precondition of their capacity to control it. Their sensory apparatus needed to be protected from assault by traffic. The chauffeur exercised and commanded the passenger's personal power without owning it. The car's extension of the driver's sensorium, so important elsewhere as the index of automotive freedom, can be recognised here as an unwanted, dubious privilege. Chauffeur and passenger collaborate in what might be called a "driving Miss Daisy" dyad: a model of interdependency that is best approached as an updated version of Hegel's famous arrested conflict between master and slave. In African American twentieth-century culture, it is of course Richard Wright's Bigger Thomas whose Fordist nihilism points towards this possibility. We should remember that his existential tragedy begins with induction into the chauffeur's role:

The night air had grown warmer. A wind had risen. He lit a
cigarette and unlocked the garage the door swung in and again
he was surprised and pleased to see the lights spring on automatically. These people's got everything he mused. He examined the car; it was a dark blue Buick, with steel spoke wheels
and of a new make. He stepped back from it and looked it over;
then he opened the door and looked at the dashboard. He was a
little disappointed that the car was not so expensive as he had
hoped, but what it lacked in price was more than made up for
in color and style.[61]

Nowadays, the figure of the chauffeur fades away because the car is no
longer a place of work. It is almost always a play space. Albert King's assembly line has slipped out of sight, along with those other topoi of residual slavery, the Killing Floor and the Chain Gang. Few workers in
North America's remaining car plants debate C. L. R. James's *Notes on
Dialectics* during their breaks or strive to apply its insights to the struggle against speedups, layoffs, and outsourcing. Workers commute long
distances, but their driving to their employment is not recognised as
part of the workday and is typically presented as a form of enforced rec-
reation.

These are the conditions under which the car has become a comfortable platform for the boomin' onboard sound systems which have done
so much to alter the soundscape of African American popular music.
That technology is celebrated in *The Source* magazine, which includes
an annual guide to the latest car audio arrayed under the chilling motto,
"A ride is a man's best friend." Automotive sound technologies are displayed alongside the alarms and immobilisers necessary to protect them
from the attention of unwanted consumers. The wattage of these mobile
sound systems is only half-seriously quantified in the distance measure of audible blocks. "'Let's just say that I spent a nice piece,' says

Usher of his CR210 car stereo with removable faceplate and six bass box speakers all by Becker/Porsche, and his two 250-watt Rockford Fosgate Punch amps. . . . Usher . . . says he's hitting about a block and a half on the Ghettometer."[62] Interestingly, the power to be heard seems to exist quite separately from the prestige and horsepower of the vehicles involved: "If you were a top music executive, what kind of whip would you be pushin'? A bangin' Benz? A luxurious Lex? How 'bout a thugged-out Hummer? Well, no matter what kind of automobile you be drivin', if you really wanted to floss, you'd better have an equally butter sound system to check out all those demos. So for all you car enthusiasts, *The Source* went out and picked the brains of the big dogs in the hip hop industry to find out just how they roll."[63] The car emerges from this as a place for listening, an intrepid, scaled-up substitute for the solipsistic world of the iPod or personal stereo, a kind of giant armoured bed on wheels that can shout the driver's dwindling claims upon the world into dead public space at ever-increasing volume.

We learned in 1999, for example, that Ronald "Slim" Williams, CEO of Cash Money Records, was the driver of a Hummer who had had his Plexiglas subwoofer enclosures sandblasted with the company logo! Slim also explained that his car contained "Sony PlayStation and Nintendo 64, a Clarion VCR, and Rosen LCD TV with tuner." The only thing he thought was missing was an automatic ignition. "I want to just push a button and start it without a key, you know?" Master P, the preeminent "rap mogul" of the late Nineties business pages, told *The Observer* that having access to the fanciest car with the loudest stereo was an essential element in how he had built up his business.[64]

A few years later, these surveys of young African American wealth and celebrity had become a regular ritual on the financial pages. As part of a *Forbes* magazine special on which rappers and hip hop producers had banked the most bucks during the previous twelve months, we learned that hip hop's top-twenty "Cash Kings" had earned $350 million during 2006. *Forbes* was particularly keen to tell its readers that Jay-Z was a "noted Mercedes-Benz buff," to quote the lyrics from "Big Pimpin'" with relish, and to reveal that he had bought his girlfriend Beyoncé a million-dollar 1959 Rolls Royce convertible for her twenty-fifth birthday. Pharell Williams was outed as the owner of a Ferrari Enzo (estimated cost: $652,000), while Busta Rhymes had to make do with a Lamborghini Murciélago Roadster, which came with a $330,000 price tag. The same model was alleged to be favoured by 50 Cent.

This sort of coverage of car culture speaks to the evolution of particular patterns of taste in cars and car paraphernalia. It communicates the consolidation of the race-specific markets which have proved extremely important at a number of points in the history of the car industry. Corporate legend has it, for example, that a distinct market for Cadillacs among "wealthy Negroes" (at a time when company policy dictated that they should not be sold the cars at all) was what had unexpectedly saved the brand from extinction during the depression of the 1930s.[65] Whether or not black buyers actually rescued that particular car company, their appetites for similar upscale products were fed by a harsh social system that prohibited displays of wealth and property by the minority of blacks who were in position to make these ostentatious gestures.

We've seen that the romance of "race" and automobility did not end there. *Forbes* quoted Michael Chatman, president of Seven Figures, a Miami-based consultancy that specialised in "multicultural marketing": "A lot of what they're selling is about aspiration. . . . If the average consumer sees Jay-Z in a Maybach, they aren't going to run out and buy one, but if they see him riding in a Maybach and wearing Rocawear, they might go out and buy some of those ancillary products."[66] The car becomes a prop in an altogether different drama. This sense of brand synergy helps to explain why media coverage of black celebrities addresses all the micro-specific problems involved in "accessorising" and personalising one's ride. We were told by *The Source* that "rims are what separates the motorists from the enthusiasts. Not only do they exhibit

personality, but a fresh set of chrome-plated wheels can be the excla-
mation point of your car's overall look. . . . 'Right now people want bigger wheels,' says Joe Smith of Butler Tires in Atlanta. 'High-end customized 18- to 20-inch newer designs.'" We learned later that he "has
sold to such notables as Erick Sermon and Chili from TLC."[67] At that
time, his hottest and most expensive wheels—by Brabus and Lorinser—
were being sold for $10,000 and $8,000 apiece, respectively.

The distinction between motorists and enthusiasts is telling. It suggests, first, that the need to personalise or "customise" a car may fall
in different patterns among different ethnic or racialised groups; and,
second, that subordinate groups might be producing elements of their
own understanding of their race-coded particularity by manipulating it.
Furthermore, it raises the uncomfortable possibility that, rather than
receiving the truths of individual or collective identity from a branded,
prestigious, or expensive object, these people are projecting their race-
thwarted individuality back into the object in ways that reply to the respectable world of official, finished consumerism in exactly the way that
50 Cent's lyrics suggested. This goes beyond simply opening up those
commodities to ongoing work, by making them into a process rather
than a closed artifact. When they speak on behalf of their owners and
users, they speak *instead of* their owners and users. Even if they are ges-
turing their official refusal of racial discipline towards power, it will not
prevent the whirlpool of consumerism from sucking them in.

It is hard to locate any crumbs of hope in the more pathological results of this process of surrender, elaborated in places like *Vibe* magazine:

> This is "my big black truck" that I sing about in "This Is How
> We Do It," says Montell Jordan as his '95 GMC Suburban ac-
> celerates through the slow-moving Los Angeles traffic. At the
> time of his first single, Jordan's road monster was just a fan-
> tasy. . . . But once that single hit No. 1, . . . and once the $64,000

loan he'd taken to attend Pepperdine University was paid off,
the truck of his dreams drove into his life. "Off the lot, the
truck only cost forty thousand, tops," explains Jordan, his size-
12 Gucci loafer pressing the gas. "And then another forty to get
it customized." "Customized" is too tame a word. This vehicle
(which is insured for a million bucks) is just plain macked out.
There's a TV and VCR with infrared headsets and an onboard
video library, . . . temperature controlled cup-holders, a mini-
humidor stocked with a selection of fine cigars, a digital com-
pass and thermometer mounted on the rearview mirror,
leather captain's chairs in front and back, plus invisible speakers cut into soundproof walls. Not all the customizing is for
comfort's sake: Jordan invested in turbocharged engine, Lamborghini brakes, PIAA purple halogen headlamps, and a roof
rack for his snowboard. . . . Any thieves scheming on the GMC
jiggmobile are sure to be stymied by a security system that can
shut off the engine via satellite.[68]

The path blazed during the 1990s by reportage of that type was consolidated in the founding of *DUB* magazine by the Californian-Japanese-
Hungarian entrepreneur Myles Kovacs and his partners in 2000. Since
then, he has built up a multimillion-dollar enterprise around the "urban car scene" which includes high-end car customisation (for clients
like David Beckham), print, computer games, toys, custom wheels, and
corporate consulting on issues related to car culture (for companies
such as Honda, Chrysler, Coca Cola, Pepsi, and Procter and Gamble).
Newsweek, which profiled Kovacs in 2005, described him as "embody-
ing the idea of blending different worlds." He was quoted as explaining,
in the characteristically race-coded idiom of corporate-speech that *DUB*
and its various offshoots were "not just urban culture. . . . This is pop
culture." *DUB* has worked closely with MTV, which also employed Kovacs
to produce "cribs" when automobiles were prominently featured. The

same article explained that he had been tutoring Detroit's ensuited car execs on the difference between "posing and getting real." Kovacs himself explained that he was "trying to educate people about getting close to young consumers without going 'Yo, yo, yo.'" The success of the *DUB* project was put down to the fact that "unlike typical car mags there are no reviews or criticism. Kobe Bryant and Mike Tyson have been cover boys with nary a mention of their legal difficulties. 'We treat people like human beings,' says Kovacs, 'and give them the privacy they deserve.'" Kovacs' interview concluded with the news that he intended to make *DUB* into the new *Playboy:* "a launching pad for a lifestyle. . . . 'It's all about aspiration,' he says. 'Instead of chain-link fences, they need to show the Hamptons.'"[69]

The same philosophical approach had provided the foundation for "Pimp My Ride," MTV's own custom-car show, which articulated their homage to the timeless culture of the U.S. high school parking lot. From its inception in 2003, the show won the channel a large international audience. The format has been copied in Brazil, New Zealand, Italy, Germany, Canada, France, the Netherlands, and the U.K., as well as appearing on MTV Arabia. The original show has also been sold worldwide.

Even in these anodyne forms, the planetary reach of the African American vernacular has meant that globalising black culture has been repeatedly oriented towards North American standards, desires, and passions. These inclinations cannot be easily separated from the dynamic, depressing pattern of U.S. race consciousness and racialised hierarchy. One result of this can be seen in the export of a car culture in which automobiles became more than simply either tools or signs. Once black history and experience were understood and widely experienced as largely urban if not always metropolitan phenomena, shifting patterns of car ownership, car use, and car fascination articulated political and moral problems around the constitution of community and the integrity of its own subaltern public world. Cars and their antisocial sociality redrew the line between public and private, impacted profoundly upon gender relations, illuminated class divisions, interrogated selfishness, and tested the mutuality of suburban residential locations that were increasingly remote from places where work could be found. The institution of American apartheid was closely connected to the extinction of the walking city and the consolidation of a diminished automotive citizenship—the limits of which were discovered in New Orleans as Hurricane Katrina approached the city. This alone suggests that studying car culture can help to clarify the shifting political character of twentieth-century African American movements towards justice and against the indignities of white supremacy.

Let us jump-start the concluding part of this argument by introducing another iconic figure. Bob Marley, translocal star on the planetary stage, provided the twentieth century's last effective contribution to the forms of black consciousness that could span the divisions of colonial development and speak in different but complementary ways to dispersed and remote populations. His language, political and poetic, helped to synchronise their consciousness and their own divergent analyses of local experiences with a universal rhetoric of "sufferation." Marley's itinerant consciousness and his subtle command of Rastafari "livity" (whole way of life) refined his skill with words. He remains notorious for renaming BMWs "Bob Marley Wagons" and thus, from my point of view, confirming the long-distance force of U.S. consumer culture's romances with auto-mobility and the car's technological sublime. But although he had lived in the United States, Marley came from an environment in which, as numerous reggae tunes testify, the pleasures of speed and auto-mobility were more usually experienced on two rather than four motorised wheels. Long before he capitulated to the pleasures of a "Bimma," he had been seen driving through Kingston in a secondhand Hillman Minx bought in 1968. Still less familiar is the time that Marley —who was, after all, the son of a green-card "Jamerican" and had ducked his callup papers for the Vietnam war by fleeing back to the Caribbean—

spent working in the U.S. automobile industry at the Chrysler plant in Wilmington, Delaware. The pain of that experience is most obviously audible in his song "Night Shift," but it is not only there. Like the time he spent working as a janitor in Wilmington's Dupont Hotel, it clearly conditions other aspects of his moral and political distaste for the corrupting superficiality of Babylon. I want to pause over that portrait of Marley: not the anxious, upwardly mobile driver cocooned in a shiny private shell of German techno-aesthetic excellence "accessorised" with his vanity plates, but the grumbling and disaffected worker in the car industry. It was there, in that crucible, on the seat of that forklift truck, that his acute understanding of the relationship between slavery and wage slavery was refined. Perhaps from those moments of disenchantment a twenty-first century critique of consumer capitalism might be reintroduced into the vacuum that black political thought has become?

2

Declaration of Rights

> I do not doubt that the ultimate art coming from black folk is going to
> be just as beautiful, and beautiful largely in the same ways, as art that
> comes from white folk, or yellow, or red; but the point today is that
> until the art of the black folk compels recognition they will not be
> rated as human. —**W. E. B. Du Bois (1926)**

As it became both popular and influential, the political idea of human
rights acquired a particular historical trajectory. However, the official genealogy it has been given is extremely narrow. The story of its
progressive development is often told ritualistically as a kind of ethno-
history. It forms part of a larger account: the story of the moral and legal
ascent of Europe and its civilisational offshoots. Blood-saturated histories of colonisation and conquest are rarely allowed to disrupt that tri-
umphalist tale. To make matters worse, struggles against racial or ethnic
hierarchy are not usually viewed as an important source or inspiration
for human rights movements and ideologies. Advocacy on behalf of indigenous and colonised peoples does not merit more than token discussion as a substantive factor in shaping how the idea of universal human rights developed and what it could accomplish.

A conventional chronology of human rights bolsters this narrative. It

suggests that there was a period of relative silence on these issues between the eighteenth century, when they were much discussed, and the
twentieth century, when the same concerns were revived in the shadow
of mass death by figures like H. G. Wells and André Mandelstam,
who would create the moral and legal momentum that led, in 1948, to
the U.N.'s Universal Declaration of Human Rights. Various reasons have
been advanced for the apparent muting of debate over human rights in
Europe and North America. Yet few chroniclers of human rights have
been prepared to consider the way in which any quieting of those discussions might have corresponded to Europe's imperial dominion, coincided with the struggle against racial slavery in the Americas, and
dovetailed with intensified conflict between Europeans and indigenous
peoples in many locations. Without wanting to dispute the extent of any
temporary shift away from concern with human rights or to estimate
the impact of critical commentaries on the idea of natural rights which
were articulated during the supposed interlude by figures as different as
Marx and Bentham, I think it is important to complicate this shallow
account.

It would be worthwhile to establish the impact of commentaries on
morality, law and politics, humanity, natural rights, and human rights
that derived from the transnational movement to abolish slavery and
the related struggle for women's rights. At times, political and philosophical struggles against the peculiar institution were extended into a
broader assault upon racial hierarchy which invoked an idea of universal humanity—often, though not always, religious in origin—as well as an
idea of inalienable rights.[1] This alternative could be articulated in distinctive accents that were neither bourgeois nor liberal.[2]

Recent attempts to revive colonial relations have been accompanied
by an intense pressure to revise colonial history. That dubious development has made it imperative to see the West's avowal of modern, liberal,
humanistic, and humanitarian ideas in the context of the formative encounter with native peoples whose moral personality and humanity had

long been placed in doubt. Generating an alternative to the simplistic
accounts of moral progress involved in this view of civilisation's forward
march requires that we focus on how different kinds of commentary on
issues like shared humanity and common rights developed. How did
they speak to particular historical conjunctures and conflicts, and how
did they shape uneven moral sensibilities that could blur the formal
lines of political ideology, especially when geo-political and economic
advantage were at stake? These questions became acute when European
political and economic domination was made intelligible in terms that
linked the imperatives of history and nature under the sign of race.[3]

An alternative, critical approach requires seeing not just how all-
conquering liberal sensibilities evolved unevenly into considerations of
human rights, but how a range of disputes over and around the idea of
universal humanity—its origins, its hierarchies, and varying moral and
juridical dispositions—were connected to struggles over race, slavery,
and imperial rule, and how they in turn produced positions that in some
cases would be narrated and claimed later as liberal.

The difficult enterprise involved in responding to the revisionist
pressure must also be able to accommodate the ironies involved in what
Mahmood Mamdani calls "rights talk,"[4] which seems always to have
been entangled with debates over who could qualify for recognition as
a rights-bearing subject in a rights-bearing body. This orientation necessitates a genealogy for human rights that differs from the usual one.[5]
It should begin with the history of conquest and expansion, and must be
able to encompass the debates over how colonies and slave plantations
were to be administered.[6] At its most basic, this agonistic, cosmopolitan enterprise must incorporate the contending voices of Bartolomé de
Las Casas and Juan Ginés de Sepúlveda. It should be able to analyse the
contrapuntality of Hobbes's *Leviathan* with England's Navigation Acts
and illuminate the relationship between Locke's insightful advocacy on
behalf of an emergent bourgeoisie and his commitment to the improv-
ers' doctrine of the *vacuum domicilium* (vacant land waiting to be settled

and cultivated). That outlook was revolutionary with regard to England's feckless aristocracy, but fatal to the indigenous inhabitants of any territory judged empty or insufficiently worked.[7]

Focusing on that combination of progress and catastrophe yields a view of what would become liberal tradition moving on from its seventeenth-century origins in a style of thought that was partly formed by and readily adapted to colonial conditions.[8] Later, it would become anchored in an anthropology that was addressed to the consequences of European conquest and shaped decisively by imperial ambitions. Concern with the Human, with race and with species, should therefore be seen as part of a revolution in European planetary consciousness.[9] It became self-conscious and was refined during the nineteenth century amidst the intellectual ferment created by the writings of Lyell and Darwin. The idea of natural hierarchy was an intrinsic ingredient.[10] Humanity—like history, historicality, and historicity—would be monopolised by Europeans, whose imperial obligations revealed to them their welcome role as cogs in metaphysical and commercial machinery driven by the forces of nature on the one hand and those of history on the other. After Darwin, it would become clear that natural mechanisms which ensured the survival of the fittest could mediate the historical and economic conflicts between nations, peoples, and races, as well as among species.

This is a roundabout way of saying that the history of Europe's colonial crimes and of the applied raciology that warranted them cannot stand outside the genealogy we create for human rights. Their inclusion emphasises the unevenness with which the idea of those rights emerged. The development of human rights cannot therefore either be plausibly or usefully narrated as a tidy sequence of waves that corresponds to the American, French, and Russian revolutions and the U.N.'s Declaration of Human Rights.

An obstinate attachment to raciology recurs throughout this civilisationist story. It resulted in the stratification and fragmentation of humanity and made the routine callousness and brutality of colonial administration appear reasonable, even if not entirely legitimate. The lingering vestiges of this presence still quietly suggest that scholars worthy of that name would never raise the topic of racism as an object of inquiry. I introduce that prospect here with trepidation because I know that however much a myopic Europe-centredness may provide today's more complacent advocates of human rights with their comfort zone, that difficult subject cannot be avoided.

Antiracism and Human Rights

It turns out that struggles against racial hierarchy have contributed directly and consistently to challenging conceptions of the human. They have valorised forms of humanity that are not amenable to colour coding, and in complicating our approach to human sameness they may even have refused the full, obvious force of natural difference articulated as both sex and gender. These struggles have not only been utopian in character. They have shaped philosophical perspectives on the fragile universals that first came into focus on the insurgent edges of colonial contact zones, where the violence of racialised statecraft was repudiated and cosmopolitan varieties of care took shape across the boundaries of culture, civilisation, language, and technology.[11] Those tendencies can be imagined to culminate in twentieth-century demands for a variety of humanism that would be disinclined to overlook Europe's colonial crimes.[12]

Theorising this alternative corresponded to ideas of political agency which arose among thinkers like Frantz Fanon, Léopold Sédar Senghor, and Amílcar Cabral—all of whom adapted the moral standpoints of anti-Fascism and official, Nazi-centred antiracism to the pursuit of national liberation by colonial peoples. A similar sensibility was evident in the long campaign against Apartheid and would be imprinted in its various successor projects in Palestine and elsewhere. With those morally charged post- and anticolonial battles in mind, I want to argue that if we wish to understand the dead spots in the rickety structure of grand, liberal tradition, and if we wish to make sense of the recurrence of its old weaknesses, which have been apparent to critics for a very long time, there is no choice but to turn our attention directly towards the problem of racial hierarchy. We must be able to analyse its practical institutionalisation in the form of colonial government, and must be prepared to understand its complex connections both to nationalist thought and to the political and juridical architecture of national states. We must also direct attention towards the imperial record of belligerent civilisationism and its projection of race as a key category in politics, economics, and culture until the aftermath of the Third Reich and the era of UNESCO statements.

For British people, there are many places to enter this forbidding archaeology. Apart from the long campaign to end slavery and the slave trade, England's responses to the anti-imperial rebellions in India (1857) and Jamaica (1865) remain among the best known. For those primarily concerned with the different challenges presented by African American history, politics, and culture, the critique of the humanitarian language and tacit racialisation of the U.S. Constitution delivered by David Walker in his messianic *Appeal to the Coloured Citizens of the World, but in Particular, and Very Expressly, to Those of the United States of America* (1830) supplies a symbolic starting point for generating a new genealogy.

Erecting secular demands over the foundation of a revolutionary, Pauline Christianity, Walker made the problem of black humanity and related issues of rights—political and human—intrinsic to the issue of *world* citizenship long before Du Bois picked up that rather Germanic theme. Walker's plea that blacks be recognised as belonging to the "human family" was combined with the view that their natural rights had been wrongfully confiscated in the condition of slavery, which could, as a result of their exclusion, be justly overthrown.[13] His famous address was offered to the coloured citizens of the world, but the tactical reduction of that universalist argument to the local problem of blacks' becoming full U.S. citizens soon followed.

The consequences of that change of imaginative scale can be readily seen in the equally humanist work of Frederick Douglass—particularly in his extraordinary 1852 speech on the meaning of the Fourth of July to the slave.[14] Douglass, who spoke directly to his fellow Americans in the name of their polluted national citizenship, linked his conceptions of humanity and manhood to a critique of the racially coded legal domain of the southern, slaveholding states. But his larger indictment against slavery was a cosmopolitan one in which the eloquent facts of racial slavery in the United States were judged, just as Walker had suggested, via a global comparison. They were compared with all the abuse to be found in "the monarchies and despotisms of the Old World [and in] South America." Douglass declared that "for revolting barbarity and shameless hypocrisy, America reigns without a rival," and then continued, again echoing Walker:

> Must I undertake to prove that the slave is a man? That point is
> conceded already. Nobody doubts it. The slave-holders them-
> selves acknowledge it in the enactment of laws for their gov-
> ernment. They acknowledge it when they punish disobedience
> on the part of the slave. There are seventy-two crimes in the
> State of Virginia, which, if committed by a black man (no mat-
> ter how ignorant he be), subject him to the punishment of
> death; while only two of these same crimes will subject a white
> man to like punishment. What is this but the acknowledgment
> that the slave is a moral, intellectual, and responsible being?
> The manhood of the slave is conceded. It is admitted in the
> fact that Southern statute books are covered with enactments
> forbidding, under severe fines and penalties, the teaching of
> the slave to read or to write. When you can point to any such

laws in reference to the beasts of the field, then I may consent
to argue the manhood of the slave. . . .

Would you have me argue that man is entitled to liberty?
That he is the rightful owner of his own body? You have already
declared it. Must I argue the wrongfulness of slavery? Is that
a question for Republicans? Is it to be settled by the rules of
logic and argumentation, as a matter beset with great diffi-
culty, involving a doubtful application of the principle of justice, hard to be understood? How should I look to-day, in the
presence of Americans, dividing, and subdividing a discourse,
to show that men have a natural right to freedom? Speaking of
it relatively and positively, negatively and affirmatively? To do
so, would be to make myself ridiculous, and to offer an insult
to your understanding.[15]

Douglass' political record suggests that, in demanding equality before
the law based on natural rights and exploring the relationship of debased citizenship and tainted law to racialised life, he was drawing upon
the thinking of an earlier cohort of abolitionist writers. Many of them
had, like Walker and other antislavery radicals, practiced a chiliastic
Christianity that built upon Saint Paul with incendiary consequences
which could not be limited by the rubric "antislavery." These thinkers
and activists had a wholesale transformation of U.S. society in mind.
Consider for a moment the way in which the Quaker and feminist Angelina Grimké articulated the concept of human rights in her landmark
1836 volume *Appeal to the Christian Women of the South:*

Man is never vested with . . . dominion *over his fellow man;* he
was never told that any of the human species were put *under his
feet;* it was only *all things,* and man, who was created in the image of his Maker, *never* can properly be termed a *thing,* though
the laws of Slave States do call him "a chattel personal"; *Man*

then, I assert *never* was put *under the feet of man,* by that first
charter of human rights which was given by God, to the Fathers
of the Antediluvian and Postdiluvian worlds, therefore this
doctrine of equality is based on the Bible.[16]

Grimké elaborated upon this inspired refusal of the reduction of people
to things in a memorable letter to her friend Catherine Beecher, the
older sister of Harriet Beecher Stowe. There, she connected the notion
of divinely instituted human rights to a growing sense of what it would
mean for women to acquire political rights. Famously, she continued:

> The investigation of the rights of the slave has led me to bet-
> ter understanding of our own. I have found the Anti-slavery
> cause to be the high school of morals in our land—the school
> in which human rights are more fully investigated and better
> understood and taught, than in any other. Here a great fun-
> damental principle is uplifted and illuminated, and from this
> central light rays innumerable stream all around. Human be-
> ings have *rights,* because they are moral beings: the rights of all
> men grown out of their moral nature, they have essentially the
> same rights.[17]

It is not easy to assimilate this variety of critical reflection exclusively
to the potent political traditions inherited by modern liberalism from
revolutionary France. The foregrounding of race is, for example, a fundamental and distinguishing feature, as is the suggestion that reflecting
upon the thwarted rights of the slave promotes a richer understanding of the rightslessness known by women. Here, women's experience
of subordination was not being understood analogically as yet another
form of slavery. Slavery was not only a political metaphor. A different
kind of connection was being proposed: we can learn about our own situation from studying the suffering of others which instructively resem-

bles it. This approach makes the disinterest in abolitionism shown by
today's chroniclers of human rights struggles all the more perplexing.

Of course, the battle to appropriate the language and political morality of the rights of man was a long one which had overlapped with the
crusade against slavery for some time. That campaign can be thought of
as having to rework the assumptions that had led to articulating the unthinkable prospects of black citizenship and black humanity in the form
of those ancient rhetorical questions immortalised in Mr. Wedgewood's
porcelain: "Am I not a Man and a brother?" "Am I not a Woman and
a sister?" The liberatory recognition solicited by those inquiries was
pitched against the corrosive power of racial categories. They asked that
the social divisions signified by phenotypical difference be set aside in
favour of a more substantive human commonality. This commonality
promised an alternative conception of kinship and could deliver a world
purged of injustice in general, and racial hierarchy in particular.

The sentimentality that is perceived to underpin this position has
been under attack for decades. In politics, it has been judged to be a
corrosive and antidemocratic force, and in art and literature it is associated above all with kitsch. James Baldwin's famous and tenden-
tious definition captured the force of these charges in his decidedly
twentieth-century assault on *Uncle Tom's Cabin:* "Sentimentality, the ostentatious parading of excessive and spurious emotion, is the mark of
dishonesty, the inability to feel; the wet eyes of the sentimentalist betray
his aversion to experience, his fear of life, his arid heart; and it is always, therefore, the signal of secret and violent inhumanity, the mask of
cruelty."[18]

This hostility and mystification also had a theoretical moment. It can
be connected to the righteous repudiation of humanism which was common among "poststructuralist" and leftist thinkers during the Cold War
years. To account for the origins of that antihumanism is beyond the
scope of the present argument, but we should note emphatically that it
does not follow the paths developed by post-1945 critics of liberal hu-

manism, whose hostility to that doctrine included its relationship to the history of colonialism, imperialism, and racism.

In his book *Human Rights and Empire*, a notable recent contribution to discussion of these problems, the jurist Costas Douzinas cites Freud's comments (in the essay "A Child Is Being Beaten") about the impact of *Uncle Tom's Cabin* and its sly and submerged erotics of suffering on the unconscious minds of the psychoanalyst's Viennese patients.[19] We should not, of course, deny the complexity of any remote identification with the suffering slave, and we must be prepared to be harsh on any variety of connection that involves a simple and immoral substitution of the comfortable reader or perverse spectator for the vulnerable victim. Yet the outright dismissal of any useful outcome from familiarity with the suffering of others should itself be questioned. Luc Boltanski and a number of others have lately begun the work of salvaging sentiment and empathy from disrepute by establishing the history of how those emotions have been debated.[20] They have done so by altering the philosophical terms within which those discussions have been conducted and by addressing the problems surrounding what Arendt called the "politics of pity." Against her argument in *On Revolution*, I take the view that compassion is not doomed to remain an ungeneralisable and antipolitical sympathy with one particular person. If we are to pursue the implications of Arendt's stance, it seems important to connect her criticism of compassion in politics with her own inability to grasp the historical and moral dynamics of the civil rights movement and its conduct in Little Rock.[21]

There are a number of ways in which strategies premised upon emotional communication, psychological identification, and the formation of moral communities might open up possibilities for change achieved through social and political mobilisation. The structures of feeling that promote that outcome might also have been registered in European cultures and societies in positive ways. Indeed, the dissemination and refinement of an idea of the human which was incompatible with racial hierarchy might already have been one result of that kind of sentimental contact across the colour line.

Freud's observation about the effects of Harriet Beecher Stowe's mode of political storytelling on his patients is interesting, but it is invoked by Douzinas only as a cautionary tale. Any remote identification with the suffering slave becomes tainted by its psychological origins and by what we might call, borrowing from a different philosophical idiom, bad faith. These days, however, the urge to dismiss peremptorily the prospect of any authentic human connection across those carefully selected and supposedly impermeable lines of absolute and always singular "identity"—class, culture, colour, gender, and sexuality—can serve its own dubious psychological and political purposes. That depressing pseudo-political gesture supplies an alibi for narcissistic quiescence and resignation to the world as it is. Timid and selfish responses are often justified in the names of complexity and ambivalence. Exploring a different genealogy for human rights requires us to consider more hopeful possibilities. What if Stowe's structure of sentimental feeling was instrumental in the formation of a moral collectivity and in winning recognition of the suffering humanity of the slave, whom it was no longer possible to dismiss as a brute? Through her voice and chosen genre, distinctive patterns of heteropathic identification appear to have leaked not only into Europe but further afield as well. *Uncle Tom's Cabin* composed a cosmopolitan chapter in the moral history of our world. Is all of that potential for political action and pedagogy to be damned now because campus Heideggerianism disapproves of the dubious aesthetic register in which it was initially made intelligible?

The scale of the historical and interpretive problems posed by the case of *Uncle Tom's Cabin* can merely be glimpsed here. The bibliographic note included in the repackaged 1879 edition was compiled by George Bullen, a curator of books at the British Museum. He revealed that almost three decades after its first publication, Stowe's novel had been translated into numerous languages, including Bengali, Farsi,

Japanese, Magyar, and Mandarin. Fourteen printings had been issued in the German language during the first year of publication; a year later, seventeen printings in French and a further six in Portuguese had also appeared. In Russia, the book had been recommended as a primer in the struggle against serfdom and was duly banned by the authorities. The first book to sell more than a million copies in the United States, Stowe's novel was a world-historic event when it was published. Though it cemented some deeply problematic conceptions of slave passivity, redemptive suffering, and indeed of racial type, it was also instrumental in spreading notions of black dignity and ontological depth, as well as an antiracist variety of universal humanism. This combination merits recognition as a potent factor in the circulation of a version of human rights that racial hierarchies could not qualify or interrupt.

The example of Stowe draws attention to issues which would reappear throughout the nineteenth century as part of struggles to defend indigenous peoples, to improve the standards of colonial government, and to reform the immorality and brutality of the imperial order. This activity was not always altruistically motivated. Some people feared that the corruption and maladministration that characterised colonial societies might infect the metropolitan hubs. Just as during slavery the consciences of the powerful, and the political and juridical traditions that guided them, had to be protected and kept as clean as possible. Nonetheless, a tradition of cosmopolitan reflection on racial hierarchy and injustice did emerge.

How the same themes were developed in the period after the end of slavery is evident from the work of the campaigning journalist Ida B. Wells, who undertook a European tour in support of the struggle against lynching as a mode of political administration in the postbellum southern states. Her lucid discussion of the paradoxical force of "lynch law" and its relationship to the South's racialised penal system, which had, in effect, continued the practice of slavery after its formal abolition, included photographic images of lynching—graphic forms of evidence

that might also be charged in a "Baldwinian" manner with sentimentality.[22] Yet in circulating those photos, she was seeking more than a ne-
farious identification with the victims of brutality. Wells appreciated the
pressure that a global public could bring to bear upon her native land
with regard to this injustice. Accordingly, she styled the relevant section of her argument, in Walkerian terms, as an "appeal from America
to the world": "The entire American people now feel, North and South,
that they are objects in the gaze of the civilized world and that for every
lynching humanity asks that America render its account to civilization
and itself."[23] The constellation of writings produced by these critical
commentators on racism, justice, and humanity needs to be recon-
structed with care and in far greater detail than is possible here. Nonetheless, we can see that they comprise a tradition of reflection on and
opposition to racial hierarchy that, even now, has the power not only to
disturb and amend the official genealogy provided for human rights, but
also to rework it entirely around the tropes of racial difference.

Allied with parallel insights drawn from other parts of the colonial
world, these interventions contribute to a counter-history that prefigures the contemporary conundrum of rights and their tactical deployment. This neglected work remains significant because debate within
the field is increasingly reduced to an unproductive quarrel between ju-
rists who are confident that the world can be transformed by a better set
of rules, and gleeful skeptics who can identify the limits of rights talk
but are almost always disinterested in racism and its metaphysical capacities.

Thinkers like Wells were alive to what we now call a deconstructive
approach. They identified problems with rights talk and saw the way
that racial difference mediated the relationship of that lofty rhetoric to
brutal reality. They grasped the limits of rights-oriented institutional
life empirically, and saw how rights claims entered into the battle to extend citizenship. But their vivid sense of the power of racism meant that
the luxury of any casual antihumanism could not be entertained. They

wished to sustain the human in human rights and to differentiate their own universalist aspirations from the race-coded and exclusionary humanisms which spoke grandly about all humanity but made whiteness into the prerequisite for recognition. Their alternative approach required keeping the critique of race and racism dynamic and demanding nothing less than the opening of both national and world citizenship to infra-human beings like the Negro.

Critical assessments of the complicity between shallow rights talk and routinely brutal regimes of unfreedom induced Grimké, Wells, and the rest to try to appeal against racism and injustice in humanity's name. Their commentaries might even represent the quickening of the new humanism of which Fanon would speak years later. The movement these commentators created and mobilised persisted into the twentieth century, when new causes and opportunities would repeat and amplify its critique of racialised political cultures and legal orders.

Yet Another Modernity

The modern world of black politics can be triangulated by the history of three sovereign states: Haiti, Liberia, and Ethiopia. The Caribbean republic was forged by a successful eighteenth-century uprising of slaves and free blacks. The rebels blended Enlightenment ideals into a movement which drew its militant, transformative energy from the spirit world of voodoo. Later, in the nineteenth century, the West African country would grow out of the slaves' embattled return to the continent from which their foreparents had been stolen away. The returnees were determined to demonstrate that they too could build and govern a national state and thus vindicate their contested humanity and historicality. The third of these states, Ethiopia, was one of the world's oldest countries, an ancient power distinguished by its biblical pedigree. During the late nineteenth and early twentieth centuries, its independence and territorial integrity were made into objects of pan-African consciousness by a series of wars with the invading Italians. The country's preeminent position in the political imagination of African and African-descended peoples derives from the conflict with Mussolini's Fascism and from the globalisation of black solidarity that it generated. Here, too, issues of human rights would become relevant. During the 1930s, that battle against colonial invasion was fought not only in the Ethiopian province of Tembien and the town of Maychew, but also on the streets of New York City among the dispersed affiliates of Africa and Italy.[24]

Haile Selassie had been crowned emperor in 1930. His appearance as ruler coincided with a tide of Ethiopianist political sentiment across the black Atlantic world, which had been galvanised into action by the revolution in Russia and by Marcus Garvey's United Negro Improvement Association (UNIA). The pageantry and military discipline of the Garvey movement had restored pride and dignity to New World black populations scarred by racism. Garvey saw the long-term future of those people through the eventual goal of return to Africa, and looked upon that aim as the focal point of restoration and uplift for the descendants of slaves. Selassie's embattled feudal kingdom was therefore of the highest importance diplomatically, geo-politically, and symbolically. Its worldly significance contrasted sharply with its internal instability, inequalities, and regional and ethnic divisions.

Ethiopia had not only maintained its beleaguered independence for centuries; it had also joined the League of Nations, where the new emperor pleaded for support against the Italian invaders. That war is remembered primarily for marking the start of humanitarian action by the International Committee of the Red Cross (ICRC) and for the invaders' carefree deployment of chemical weapons, which were rained down on Selassie's country by Mussolini's aircraft in violation of Italy's treaty obligations. Mustard gas was used against civilian populations judged to be a verminous part of the natural rather than the historical world.[25]

For the wider black public that was born into the era of the newsreel and the radio broadcast, these modern horrors dramatised the political and economic dynamics of racism and imperialism. Selassie was identified as a potent symbol of hope, freedom, and resistance against colonial domination. Under his guidance, Ethiopia would be a founding member of the United Nations and of the Organisation of African Unity. However he treated his own subjects, the country's world-famous ruler aspired to be something of a moderniser. He was one of the first political thinkers inclined to try to imagine a postcolonial future for the whole continent.

After the Nazis rose to power in 1933, their anti-Jewish policies were also discussed by the League of Nations. A plenary session of its assembly was addressed by the Greek jurist Antoine Frangulis, who spoke there as a representative of the Haitian government. He unsuccessfully proposed the establishment of an international convention on human rights under the league's auspices, and argued that a generalisation of rights held in common by all people would be the best possible way to address the vulnerable predicament of Germany's Jews.[26] The proposal was not accepted. The United States was said to be opposed to any thing that might affect the integrity of their system of racial segregation, while the British and French governments were alert to the implications of this change of policy for the administration of their imperial territories.[27]

Bearing in mind the contemporary echoes of that conflict between moral principle and colonial statecraft, we face the challenge of maintaining and perhaps refining critical work in an unstable field that retains investments in the explanatory capacity of race as an abstraction, even when the nature of that abstraction has moved away from nineteenth-century bio-logic and towards newer kinds of political anatomy. It bears repeating that the attachment to race has a habitual partner in the scholastic refusal of agonistic humanism.

The counter-narrative of human rights we require is evident in opposition to racial orders, in the struggles of indigenous peoples, and in the post- and anticolonial pursuit of liberation from imperial domination. It can furnish an extensive commentary on the effects of racism in securing the alienation of humanity. Taken together, those struggles contribute to a culture of freedom sourced from deep within the experience of objecthood. All of them resist the process by which a human being is reduced to a thing. For descendants of slaves, they summon the history of being locked away from literacy on pain of death, confined in a place where cognition—thinking—was not a special door to doubt, method, and modern being but rather a shortcut to the radical vulnerability of nonbeing and *social* death for people whose infra-human status meant they could be disposed of with impunity.

This profane history can furnish contemporary discussion with interpretive and ethical resources which we can use to orient ourselves, now that the "human" in the idea of human rights stands in urgent need of elaboration. If the idea of universal humanity is to become plausible —perhaps for the first time—it will need to be endowed with new content distinguishable from the vapid, race-friendly fillings it was given by Cold War liberalism and more recently by the belligerent humanitarianism of the "war on terror." The genealogy of human rights we produce from considerations of race hierarchy and raciology can assist us with that task.

Scholastic writing has, by and large, remained disinterested in racial discourses, divisions, and hierarchies. So whatever those formations might reveal about the ideology and acquisition of human rights has not often been considered worth investigating. Instead, the history of the race idea gets allocated to ever more esoteric academic specialisms and, if the history of *racism* appears at all, it is principally a history of racism's many victims, which is usually invoked as an act of Europe-centred piety that may also be open to the accusation of sentimentality.

These lapses represent a missed opportunity, which is compounded by the fact that the rise of almost exclusively literary postcolonial studies means that histories of racialised government, law, and politics receive scant attention. Very few writers have been bold enough to break the complicity which produces this almost-silence, to approach the metaphysical potency of racism, and to become engaged by what the history of its expressions shows about the constitution of sovereign power, the diminution of justice, and the functional articulation of rationality with irrationality. These rare figures are an odd collection of humanist and antihumanist voices that ranges across the spectrum of formal politics.[28] It would seem that the desire to understand the relationship of race and racism to politics and power was an unorthodox impulse long before the industrialisation of genocidal killing made it an urgent matter.

Political Correctness

Academic fashions have been greatly affected by a fear of being dismissed as politically correct. The rise of securitocracy is also placing a new burden on higher education.[29] In that climate, even the most embattled fields of inquiry can get taken over by timid work. The study of the body can, for example, easily get reduced to a generic enterprise. The ability to focus on which particular bodies are most at risk and the conditions in which they are produced as objects of intrusive, violent attention can be lost. It becomes difficult to address the diverse ways in which the operations of racial discourse make those bodies meaningful—always *in relation* to each other. Similar conceptual and political problems occur when racism and nationalism are allowed to drift apart. Then, the racialisation of war and law is retained as an overspecialised topic relevant only to a few exceptional places characterised by openly racialised polities and forms of citizenship that, in turn, institutionalise the patterns of exclusionary inclusion which race hierarchy facilitates and renders acceptable.

    The reluctance to consider racism as anything more or less than ideology in general, or to see racial difference as anything other than a straightforward effect of nature, seems to me an extension of an older pattern in which mechanistic assumptions about progress, nationality, and survival were overdetermined by and made congruent with various forms of racial theory, usually as an accompaniment to conquest and expropriation. George Mosse's genealogies of race, nation, and masculinity, Norbert Elias' monumental studies of the civilising process, and Michel Foucault's explorations of power and the body might be cited here, along with Adorno's post-1945 work, as counter-evidence. Their contributions all reveal the stimulation that derived, unexpectedly, from the need to bear witness to mass killing and confront the continuing menace of Hitlerism and its imitators. Those thinkers generated new forms of knowledge from their investigations of the Third Reich. Their work was done best when the colonial precursors of those atrocities were acknowledged. It created the sociology of the body and altered approaches to power—but apart from rare moments like those few tantalising sentences at the end of the first volume of Foucault's *History of Sexuality,* this variety of work premised upon opening out the "never again" injunction and moving it away from any narrow, ethnic proscription was always oblique about its relationship to those twentieth-century horrors. None of these writers was able or willing to place them inside the broader historical framework of colonial statecraft that they seem, increasingly, to demand. That task fell first to Hannah Arendt, and has in some aspects been continued in the less historically inclined work of Giorgio Agamben.

Agamben identified the concentration camp as the "nomos of the political space in which we are still living."[30] As part of an exhilarating enquiry into what the camp represents institutionally, juridically, and historically, he has criticised approaches to understanding spaces of exception and their social relations that strive to deduce their essence from accounts of what happened there. He suggests that it is more productive to invert that line of enquiry and ask instead: "What is a camp, what is its juridico-political structure, that such events could take place there?" The camp's displacement of the city from its traditionally central place in political philosophy provides the key to a wholly novel and deeply disturbing transformation of relationships between sovereignty, territory, and political culture: of the relationship between law and life. He notes in passing that the origins of these practices lie in colonial government and colonial war.

Today, the problem he has identified asks us to consider the difference between the colonial archive's role as a historical resource and its contribution to understanding how colonial and postcolonial crimes should be remembered and understood as part of debates over human rights. Are those past crimes to be part of the history of our present? If so, how are we going to make sense of their historicity? We need a new familiarity with the history of empire and colonial government, in order to accomplish that task.

In considering the colonial precedents for some contemporary practices, I have found it useful to borrow the phrase "useful violence" from Primo Levi. He employed it in *The Drowned and the Saved* at the very end of his examination of the gratuitous, excessive violence that characterised the concentrationary system.

Inspired by his work, by the philosophical writings of his fellow Auschwitz inmate and interlocutor Jean Améry, and by various other observers of and commentators on the pathologies of European civilisation, I aim to answer the corrosive allure of absolute sameness and purity just as they did: with a historical and moral commitment to the political, ethical, and educational potential of human *shame.* Though being ashamed may sometimes appear to overlap with sentimentality or even to be its result, they are different. Sentimentality blocks shame's productivity, its slow, humble path towards virtue. Shame arises where identification is complicated by a sense of responsibility. Sentimentality offers the pleasures of identification in the absence of a feeling of responsible attachment. I hope to show that a universal shame can also be significant in the political opportunities now being opened up by a critical postcolonial commentary on human rights.

Améry was an eloquent proponent of what he called "radical human-ism." Through discovering his Jewishness under the impact of some-body's fist, but more especially as a result of having been tortured by the Nazis, he developed a keen interest in a politics of dignity which could answer the governmental actions that brought racial hierarchy to dismal life. Perhaps for that very reason, he found through his postwar reading of Fanon that "the lived experience of the black man . . . corresponded in many respects to my own formative and indelible experience as a Jewish inmate of a concentration camp." He continues:

> I too suffered repressive violence without buffering or miti-gating mediation. The world of the concentration camp too was a Manichaean one: virtue was housed in the SS blocks, profligacy, stupidity, malignance and laziness in the inmates' barracks. Our gaze onto the SS-city was one of "envy" and "lust" as well. As with the colonized Fanon, each of us fanta-sized at least once a day of taking the place of the oppressor. In the concentration camp too, just as in the native city, envy ahistorically transformed itself into aggression against fellow inmates with whom one fought over a bowl of soup while the whip of the oppressor lashed at us with no need to conceal its force and power.[31]

Levi shared with Améry and Fanon a commitment to extracting human-istic perspectives from the extremity he had survived in the lager. Ana-lytical insights towards that end flow freely in his writing, especially in his final work, *The Drowned and the Saved*.[32] It is a book that can be ap-proached most profitably as an examination of the *reductio ad absurdum* of key motifs in the history of the bureaucratic and military rationalities that help to define the specific attributes of modern governmentality.[33] Those qualities are seen with special clarity in government's encounters with the vulnerable figures who, outside the protection of rights but firmly under the rule of law, can be killed with impunity.

The book includes Levi's famous essay on "useless violence." It lies at the centre of his exploration of civilisation's inner tensions and the implication of decivilising racial divisions that are not to be dialectically resolved into a reconfigured narrative of progress. He offers a luminous treatment of the spectacular brutality that, according to standards of rational reflection, appears at first to be without purpose. He concludes with the notion that what he calls the "outrage motive" intruded into and compromised the more familiar mechanisms of the profit motive, which were not altogether absent from the social world of his lager where slave labour was a routine supplement to the procedures of the adjacent death factory. His analysis of this need for outrage delivers us to a critical and historical engagement with racial metaphysics. The subordination of profit to outrage was a sign that the power of racism and the order of race-hierarchy were active.

Building on this insight from Levi, I want to pursue the proposition that racism has a distinctive and substantive agency; and, further, that focusing on the point where the colonial archive articulates with the West's "internal" dynamics helps to make that agency recognisable in the postcolonial present. This observation may, I suppose, be thought contentious, perhaps even vulgar, but I hope it is not trivial. It bears repetition that the post-1945 forces of national liberation were marshaled by many who, like Fanon, Senghor, and Dedan Kimathi had imbibed a distinctive political morality through deployment in the war against fascism. Their subsequent attempts to adapt that ethical system, so that it would legitimise anticolonial resistance and in some cases explain the need for armed struggle, all involved arguments of this type. Their perspectives still cut deeply into the problems of how we understand the significance of states of exception, how we interpret the causality of genocide, and how we set about preventing the possibility of its recurrence, as well as how we answer culture talk and civilisationist common sense.[34]

That timely agenda has the additional merit of directing our attention towards two other fundamental issues. They can be conceptualised as counterpoints to Zygmunt Bauman's analysis of postmodern morality, as well as to a larger programme of critical work proceeding agonistically under the banners of human rights. This commitment can be abbreviated as a double concern with the loss of human dignity and with its recovery. There is, first, as Levi tells us, the dignity that was stripped away by the bio-political processes which systematically produced infra-humanity, for the explicit benefit of the killers, torturers, and abusers. And then there is the dignity that might, intermittently at least, be recovered by acts of narration, of storytelling, even if, as Walter Benjamin put it, they "borrow their authority from death."[35]

Let me emphasise that in Levi's exposition and enactment of this difficult problem, what appears to be a brutality without purpose can be made to disclose its secret significance. Apparently useless violence does have a value, and he suggests that it can be identified only when we consider the position of its perpetrators, who require it in order to complete their murderous tasks with the minimum of emotional and psychological disturbance.

In a memorable conclusion which divorces that particular history from any proscriptive uniqueness and shifts it into an inspiring world-historical mode, Levi raises the possibility that there exists another form of violence that he hopes will be useful in the longer run. Perhaps with his imminent suicide in mind, Levi named this variant as the self-inflicted suffering involved in inducing himself and others like him, first, "to speak of the fate of the most helpless" in their attempt to reconstruct and comprehend the alien logic of their murders and torturers, and then to move beyond that necessary but insufficient goal, into a different stance in which witnessing as psychopathology unfolds into witnessing as ethics.

At that point, talk as trauma is succeeded by talk as pedagogy and exchange. This conception of utility is something daring and unexpected which challenges Baldwin's notion of sentimentality once again. In the service not only of human rights but of a new humanism, a more elaborate conception of what I propose indelicately to call antiracist pedagogy might still be built upon it. It should not be necessary to add that the benefits of this proposed exercise can only increase if we appreciate that the opportunity has been summoned, conjured into being, in explicit opposition to the racialisation of the world.

These issues have become important in responding to the ongoing conduct of the "war on terror." The info-war has revived a recognisably colonial economy in which infra-humanity, measured against the benchmark set by civilisationism's racial standards, evaporates rights and postpones recognition indefinitely.[36] All the "third things"[37] that race thinking assembles between animal and human are best administered as living waste under the flexible governance produced by special emergency rules and exceptional or martial procedures, in which the law is suspended in the name of the law. An assumption of racial hierarchy is not inferred in this process; it is integral to it. Yet the complexity of this association should not persuade us to dismiss the language of human rights as a sham or a fantasy.

Arendt, Foucault, Agamben, and a few others departed from the habitual professional disinterest in these matters. They have drawn from and engaged in dialogue with the theoretical reflections offered up by the movements of the enslaved and colonised, as part of their battles for independence, autonomy, and liberation. This nascent tradition has shown us aspects of how racial hierarchy entered into the process that institutionalised sovereign powers and warranted the belligerent conduct of their competitive statecraft, the management of their colonies, and eventually the forms of bio-political government that were being developed in the core metropolitan areas, where different jungles, savages, and degenerate types would be discovered.

Turning away from the political ontologies of race, class, and nation, those thinkers appealed to variants of a constructionist approach which, when applied to race, had its origins in the intersection of existentialism and phenomenology. Where racial and ethnic identities were rendered in absolutist forms in order to secure the interests of oppressed and exploited minorities, this approach was not influential. Timidity set in and the moral and political tempo of studying racism was slowed, ironically by the success of struggles against Apartheid and by the demise of the social movements created by black Americans in pursuit of substantive citizenship. The fading of those great struggles left a disturbing sense that the most radical practitioners of *historical* ontology were becoming wary of working on race and racism. Others who operate loosely in the spirit of Ian Hacking's "dynamic nominalism" headed for calmer waters: usually where the creation of gendered subjects and sexual differences could be explored. There, the complex interaction of named subjects with the institutional processes which named them could be considered without trespassing on the political sensibilities of racial and ethnic minorities who did not appreciate having their particularity deconstructed or made to appear absurd. To see this more critically, the elaboration of easy, antihumanist positions was unlikely to be disrupted by any inconvenient clamour from the vulnerable groups whose political rights had become entangled with demands for recognition as human beings in an unjust world that denied them even that protection.

The popular, academic response to the minorities' assertion of sovereignty over their experience of victimage was the dubious idea that we should all become resigned to racial orders because they are natural kinds and therefore a permanent, significant, and immutable aspect of human social and political life. Attempts to denature race, to become estranged from its obvious common sense, to focus on its dynamic constructedness and its implication within particular institutional settings, are—in the corona of identity politics, anyway—judged harshly and often thought to belong more naturally and spontaneously to the right than to the left.

The approach that Foucault pioneered—more, I think, from his political commitments than from his critique of epistemology, though they are of course connected—would not accept that the appearance of a political language of race and its growing relationship to the administration and reproduction of governmental and police powers were incidental developments: just coincidences in which the languages of natural difference and real kinds were momentarily addressed to the pragmatic challenges of colonial rule or the shifting tempo of class conflict.

Instead, Foucault suggested that the historical currency of race thinking, and its tight grip on a world of empires, could tell us something fundamental and useful about the shifting quality of political life, about the objects of government and the nature of subjection. Something like a historical ontology of the actors we know as races might then be used to illuminate all the contradictions—legal, ethical, military—of a civilising mission that had to mystify its own systematic brutality in order to be effective.

With these goals in mind, we can agree with Arendt that race talk and racial solidarities prosper where politics, political institutions, and "the political" are diminished or compromised. Yet there is a sense in which her inspirational linkage of Europe's colonial rule with its genocidal ultranationalism can be misleading.

Though Arendt is deeply interested in the relationship of the race idea to imperialism, her understanding of racism is—as we saw from her ill-judged commentary on Little Rock—more problematic. It remains comfortably and tidily ideological, rather than metaphysical; as Margaret Canovan puts it, racism for Arendt "was the spontaneous and comprehensible response of civilised men confronted with savages."[38] The consequences of this tension are strongly evident at the conclusion of Arendt's famous chapter on the decline of the nation-state and the end of the rights of man—the essay which has been so pivotal in the development of human rights scholarship.

As is well known, Arendt emphasised that rights came from national states and that the vulnerability of statelessness was compounded by rhetorical appeals to humanity. She moved rapidly from those insights to elaborate upon another problem, which resided in the fact that "the world found nothing sacred in the abstract nakedness of being human."[39] Identifying this observation explicitly with the experience of survivors of the Nazi death factories, Arendt argued that "the abstract nakedness of being human was their greatest danger." A repeated preference for the national over the natural dictated that, when people appeared outside the protection of their political community, their very humanity may have been an inducement to violence against them. "It seems," she continued, "that a man who is nothing but a man has lost the very qualities which make it possible for other people to treat him as a fellow man."[40]

Arendt misrecognises the abstractly naked human as a natural or abstractly essential human. Instead, this vulnerable figure might be described more accurately and more usefully as a racialised human: a particular, infra-human creation, rather than a specimen of the catastrophically empty humanity that she wishes to repudiate. This error corresponds to a refusal to engage racism critically.

The possibility that this abstract nakedness is not so much a cipher of insubstantial humanity as a sign of racial hierarchy in operation arises directly from the work of survivors themselves. It bears repeating that Améry recognised his experiences through reading Fanon and Levi, who interpreted brutal exercises in racial formation as conducted for the benefit of their perpetrators, and suggested that racism's capacity to reconcile rationality and irrationality was expressed in the dominance

of outrage even over profit. The infra-human victims were made to perform the subordination that race theory required and anticipated, but
that their bodies did not spontaneously disclose. Levinas, who offered a
very different but dazzlingly insightful diagnosis of similar questions in
the years before the Third Reich, stated the fundamental problem in a
1934 article for the journal *Esprit:*

> How is universality compatible with racism? The answer—to
> be found in the logic of what first inspires racism—involves a
> basic modification of the very idea of universality. . . . But here
> we return to well-known truths. We have tried to link them to a
> fundamental principle. Perhaps we have succeeded in show-
> ing that racism is not just opposed to such and such a particu-
> lar point in Christian and liberal culture. It is not a particu-
> lar dogma concerning democracy, parliamentary government,
> dictatorial regime, or religious politics that is in question. It is
> the very humanity of man.[41]

Agamben's important recent interventions exhibit some of the same
failings as Arendt's account. His philosophical ambitions mean that he
sees nothing specific in the power of racial discourse or in the way that
racialised forms of law contribute to the problem of exclusionary inclusion. The specific dynamics involved in colonial war and law are absent from those metaphysical and juridical stories, from which racism
must be excluded at all costs. This is a grave oversight because, as Sven
Lindqvist has argued, an issue like the legitimacy of preemptive violence is directly linked into the parapolitical and judicial rules of racialised government which Carl Schmitt understood to be connected to the
development of European public law, particularly in relation to the colonisation of the Americas.[42]

Perhaps, like Arendt, Agamben missed something. His distinctions
between *zoe* and *bios, physis* and *polis,* pass over the intermediate figures

that arise where the rational irrationalities of race and blood are set to work. Even if we accept that at the end of this grim road lies "bare life" in the figure of the "Musselman," we are entitled to ask about the historical and geo-political stops along the way, the points of conflict, intersection, and confluence which looped colonial procedures back into the core of European social life with such dreadful results.

How does the ultimate destination represented by that bare life relate to the other forms of political ontology which have specified who may be slain with impunity in the name of racial hygiene and whose life counts for nothing? Where, for example, is the *andrapoda,* the noncitizen, the prisoner of war, or the slave represented in the figure of Aristotle's man-footed beast? Where are the alien denizens who even now function as the constitutive outside of shrinking citizenship? Where are the colonial functionaries and Malthusian rulers who engineered and manipulated famines as a way of waging war or recruited the desert itself into their calculations as to the rational mechanisms of genocide?

At the start of his rich chapter on the camp as the nomos of the modern, Agamben acknowledges the historical association of the concentration camp with the prosecution of colonial warfare. He notes that the camp was not born from ordinary or criminal law, but came instead from the strategy of "protective custody" and the state of exception. The initial colonial staging of this problem does not detain him. As soon as the fatal connection is noted, it is set aside and his larger philosophical and juridical argument resumes with a discussion of the state of exception as a bridge—he calls it a "constitutive nexus"—into the Third Reich from the ordinary judicial processes of the governments that had preceded it.

I have no major quarrels with the way his argument unfolds, though I am not convinced that the National Socialist concept of race did not involve "the identification of a certain biological body." His haste in passing over the specificities of the question of racism, its political ontologies, its legal ordering under the sign of the national state, and its larger epistemological shape interests me because it seems to be symptomatic of more than a philosopher's refusal of history. Colonial statecraft, colonial government, and the legitimate deployment of forms of law and power which would be unacceptable in other locations all drop out of his important reflections.

Arendt and Agamben are linked by their apparent distaste for analysing racism, but also by their complex and critical relations to the idea of the human. This combination of positions can facilitate hostility to the project of human rights, which is dismissed for its inability to face the political and strategic processes from which all rights derive and for a related refusal to address the analytical shortcomings that arise from the dependence of human rights on an expansion of the rule of law— which incidentally can be shown to be fully compatible with colonial crimes.[43]

Histories of colonial power and genealogies of racial statecraft can help to explain both of these problems and to break the impasse into which the analysis of human rights has fallen. That is why antiracism remains important. It does not argue naïvely for a world without hierarchy but practically for a world free of that *particular* hierarchy which has accomplished untold wrongs.

Ida B. Wells and others have reminded us already that racial terror assumed paralegal as well as legal forms. That pattern raises the additional issue of racism's role in supplying the means of their articulation. Racial discourse can be thought as contributing to a system for making meaning that feeds the tendency to create exceptional spaces and populate them with vulnerable, infra-human beings.

Colonial battlefields gave birth to plantations, which point in turn to the legal regimes of protective custody that generated and generalised the camp as a routinely exceptional space. If the social and political force of racism is taken into account, those exceptional spaces become explicable, and racial discourses are revealed as an essential and dynamic element in their legitimation. The resulting nomos—the spatial ordering of law and power—corresponds to hierarchically ordered forms of moral personality and legal subjectivity.

The governmental dynamics of settler colonialism were also distinctive. In example after example, racial hierarchy and the domination of a large number of people by a much smaller number with a greater measure of force set up particular patterns. Law became partial, fractured, and flexible. Violence, on the other hand, was spectacular, excessive, and yet always imagined to be functional. A radical insecurity common to the colonial settler, the slaveholder, and the militarily superior extractive agent inclined them all towards the deployment of terror as a means of political administration. Their violent dramaturgies of power were routinised and ritualised to mark out the spaces in which normal rules were suspended or inapplicable.

Mick Taussig's study of the colonial administration of the Putumayo region of Colombia during the rubber boom provides one especially memorable example of procedures that typified the operation of corporate power in what he terms the colonial "space of death."[44] This was an essentially privatised military topos which, as the well-known example of the Congo Free State also reveals, existed in an ambivalent relationship to the official system of national states. Recent interest in the history of Belgian colonialism shows how important these formations are to understanding imperialism in relation to corporate power and to avowedly humanitarian state-making practice.[45]

The problems that states of exception posed for citizenship and for the language of political rights had been recognised long before they assumed twentieth-century form and Arendt made them relevant to political theory that was casting around to uncover the causality of industrialised genocide in Europe. Rosa Parks would describe her own motivation towards racial insubordination in the same familiar terms: "I had decided that I would have to know once and for all what rights I had as a human being and a citizen, even in Montgomery, Alabama."[46]

Grasping for the distinctiveness of the racial nomos, a dissident understanding of the ways in which race worked to compromise and corrupt politics could also, counter-intuitively, show that the entities we learn to name as races derive from the very racial discourse which appears to be their scientific product. The special accomplishments of racial discourse can then be explored. Its elisions, perlocutions, and performatives can become historical problems to be understood, rather than simple but enigmatic emanations pulsing out from the decisive world of biology to shape the course of history, the rhythm of culture, and the conduct of social life. In particular, we can consider the role of race and ethnic absolutism in securing the modes of inclusive exclusion that characterise what we might call the age of rendition—a period in which a combination of public and private powers, mercenaries, contractors, and securitocrats harks back to the eighteenth century.

Oppositional, antiracist practice cannot of course proceed without all the usual attention to formally political and economic matters. That acknowledgement does not dispose of the problem which resides in whether we are to accept the integrity and validity of race as a concept, and how we are to manage the contending claims made upon raciality by racism's victims as well as by its practitioners: enthusiastic and unwitting, indifferent and dogmatic. The ability to conscript the future into the service of racial equality remains pending in this choice, and so does the political success of contemporary initiatives based upon the idea of human rights. Here, we must turn in the direction of a vernacular view of human rights articulated by a different generation of intellectuals in the black Atlantic tradition.

Bob Marley, Antipolitics, and I-niversal Sufferation

Almost three decades after his premature death, Bob Marley's many recordings are still selling all over the world. His ubiquitous image suggests an immortal, uncanny presence. Across the planet, his serious, pained, and permanently youthful expression looks out from T-shirts, hats, badges, walls, and posters.

His recordings have been found in the pockets of unidentified African bodies washed up upon the beaches of Europe, to which they sought illegal entry. His digitally remastered voice still talks back to power, exploitation, and indifference with all the insolent style and complex rhetoric of a soul rebel captured in the process of becoming a dread revolutionary. That unchanging face now represents an iconic, godly embodiment of a universal struggle for justice, peace, and human rights, a prefiguration of more positive forms of global interconnection.

Marley's global visibility helps us here in a number of ways. Historically, it can be used to mark a turning point in the development of the Ethiopianist tradition, rooted in slavery, which has managed to export its particular conceptions of freedom and human rights into the furthest recesses of our planet. Politically and culturally, it embodies a decisive shift away from U.S.-centred discourses on blackness and its limits. Marley's stardom therefore represents a move into what might be termed a "Third World" mode of freedom struggle. This has been more cosmopolitan, less parochial, and far less bound up with the corporate machinery of consumer culture than the generic versions of black culture discussed briefly in the preceding chapter. It communicates the possibility that the modern colonial telos of centre and periphery is being reversed. Last, the timing of Marley's popularity has coincided with the unfolding of global immanence.[47] His words of denunciation and comfort have been able to resonate everywhere they have been heard.

Before we can assess the issues addressed by Marley's immortal art, we must face the fact that his largely posthumous success itself poses significant problems of history, politics, and cultural interpretation. Though it is rarely considered as a separate question, the ubiquity and plasticity of his virtual image shows how, during the late twentieth century, it became possible to translate fundamental ethical and political insights into a huge variety of languages, traditions, and idioms. Conventional approaches to the relationship between commerce, communication, culture, and politics have either ignored or failed to appreciate the complex character of this event. The cosmopolitan concerns—not least with human rights—that he articulated from below, in explicit opposition to the destructive, vampire forces of "Babylon System," pass unremarked upon. Marley's epiphany asks us to rethink our understanding of power and solidarity in the light of his life as a nomadic migrant worker, to say nothing of his musical achievements.

The history of Marley's continuing worldwide appeal reveals a distinctive blend of moral, spiritual, political, and commercial energies. More even than Che Guevara, whose equally iconic features do a similar kind of worldwide cultural work, and Jimi Hendrix, whose comparable immortality won his music new audiences and an amazing global reach, Marley's commercial afterlife arrived courtesy of postmodern consumer culture. Its technological resources have subdued the constraints of nature and endowed his image with virtual life-after-death in which popularity and sales can continue to grow. They seem to have increased faster after Marley's image was purged of any embarrassing political residues that might make him into a threatening or frightening figure. The results of this innovative sales and public-relations strategy were brought home when, in 1999, *Time* magazine pronounced the album *Exodus* to be the most important pop recording of the twentieth century!

The glamour of the primitive had been set to work. It reanimated Bob and increased the power of his music to seduce. The postmodern magic that manufactured his immortality also required his moral and political legacies to be both purified and simplified. An aura of rebel authenticity was projected, not to validate his complex parapolitical aspirations or demotic intransigence, but to invest the arresting music with a mood of carefully calculated transgression designed to make it salable and appealing. A thrilling and exotic racial otherness was invoked and contained where that music was made to supply an affecting background to essentially boring and empty activities like shopping and getting stoned. The difference that race made increased the gulf between Marley's memory and his remote "crossover" audiences and helped to manage the resulting experiential gap, so that their pleasure in consuming him and his work was somehow enhanced by the thrill of vicariously inhabiting his youthful rebel persona.

Marley's presence in global popular culture involves far more than just an important reminder of the power of the technologies which underpinned the phantasmagoria of cultural simulation. To make sense of his stature, we have to understand the historical conjuncture of culture, politics, and technology that framed his stardom but that, though necessary, is insufficient to provide an explanation of his popularity. There is more to this worldwide appeal than a clever video-based resurrection and the projection of his heroic personality so that militant Ethiopianism could be exchanged for the routine profile of pop notoriety. There is something more to his unbounded appeal than a domestication of the alien other and the accommodation of an unruly Third World inside the seductions of corporate multiculturalism. Something gritty and important remains to be considered, even if we dismiss the presentation of exotic racial difference as a spectacle and a powerful marketing device in the global business of selling records, tapes, CDs, videos, and the other merchandise now available at www.BobMarley.com and catch-a-fireclothing.com. That surplus inevitably directs our attention towards Marley's utopian politics, and in particular to the timely manner in which he articulated the issues of human rights and justice.

For the moment, analysis of any formal innovations in his musical attempt to reconcile Caribbean reggae with North American rhythm and blues must take third place behind the significance of his strange immortality, and the fact of its role as the site of a revolution in the structure of the global markets for new kinds of cultural commodities. As the posthumous popularity of the music increased, the gravity of Marley's dissidence remained at odds with the commercial vitality of the myths —footballer, stud, freedom fighter—that were intertwined with his uncanny celebrity. In other words, the same spectral image which made Bob into the global patron of rebels, resisters, and dissenters transcended its function as the source of his Third World glamour. The purchase of all sorts of objects far removed from the simple needs and humble, ascetic life of the Rastaman that he may have aspired to be before he wandered down the path to fame would no longer count as acts of rebellion. At that point, Marley can be judged to have become a brand, as well as a symbol of resistance and resilience. Yet his presence was invested with a saintly quality that is at odds with the branding dynamic. Canonised, he retains a unique moral authority that is drawn from profane and openly oppositional sources. This precious quality is what helps to transmit resources of hope into a future different from the one brought to mind by supposedly limitless consumerism and the alienated social relations that he dismissed as a "rat race."

Still, we need to explore the utopia that was summoned by his music and by the revolutionary post- and anticolonial imaginings of his poetry. Thankfully, that dreamland is not delimited by a proscriptive ethnic wrapper or racial "health warning" in which encounters with otherness are presented as dangerous to the well-being of one's own singular identity. Music and instrumental competence have to be learned and practised before they can be made to communicate convincingly. Remembering this patient preparatory labour should restrict their transformation into ciphers of authentic, absolute particularity. Perhaps also, in the tainted but nonetheless powerful imagery of Bob Marley's global triumph, we can begin to discern the force of an alternative, postracial identity based not on some automatic or pregiven sameness, but on will, inclination, mood, and affinity. Bob's lyrics do more than remind us of the difficult goal involved in making the colour of skin no more significant than the colour of eyes. They also admonish anybody who hesitates before the weighty existential responsibility which comes with knowing that—contrary to even the most awful appearances—you do rule your destiny.

The translocal power of this dissenting voice conjures with these uncomfortable possibilities and starts to celebrate a chosen, recognisably political idea of kinship that is all the more valuable for its distance from the disabling assumptions of mechanical solidarity based on either shared blood or shared land. From this perspective, solidarity has to be won. Ideally, it will be created in the real-time social act of reasoning, and then consolidated in the enactment of revelation.

The balance between memory and creativity, between the contending obligations to know the past and to act judiciously in the present, can be adjusted—and thus the meaning of Marley starts to change. Consumer culture loses control of his ghost. We can begin to appreciate that he was not just a symbol of the late twentieth-century universality that globalised and popularised the ideal of human rights, galvanising dispersed people into a tide of feeling that was sometimes powerful enough to make governments pause. We see also that his interventions actually helped to bring a novel solidary network into being. It is not exactly clear what the political significance of this formation may be. But it will not be easily compatible either with a securitocracy or other totalitarian forms of political community. This aspect of Marley's legacy was confirmed a few years after his death from cancer in 1981, when the Wailers' famous song "Get Up Stand Up" (co-written by Marley and his sometime bandmate Peter Tosh) was adopted by Amnesty International as the anthem for their worldwide tour in support of the programme outlined in the Universal Declaration of Human Rights. That historic gesture bestowed a degree of respectability on Marley and confirmed the significance of inter- and transcultural developments which had begun spontaneously long before he died.

Borrowing the language of rights was by no means an unusual choice among the Rastafari musicians and performers who made the 1970s into a special period in the history of Jamaican music. "Get up and fight for your rights my brothers / Get up and fight for your rights my sisters" was the influential chorus of "Declaration of Rights," a popular 1968 tune written and sung by the Abyssinians, another Impressions-influenced vocal trio who had been contemporaries of the Wailers on Coxsone Dodd's Studio One label, where they recorded initially under the name of Carlton and the Shoes. That year, Studio One had also released "Equal Rights," by the Heptones, a second influential group who had been producing innovative material under Coxsone's direction. Their anthem did not treat human rights directly, and seems to have been more influenced by the prophetic aspirations of the recently martyred Martin Luther King Jr., but it legitimised the formulation and articulation of black liberation goals in a language of rights. Jamaican music was starting to register the impact of African American civil rights struggles transmitted in song by performers like Syl Johnson and Nina Simone. Yet the famous 1960 study of the Rastafari movement in Kingston, Jamaica, carried out by the University of the West Indies, had made no mention of human rights as a concept that was of concern to the Ethiopianists.[48] It is certainly not a biblical notion, nor was it part of the largely Victorian rhetorical repertory of Marcus Garvey and the UNIA. The poetics of rights seems to have found its way into reggae via the eloquent, worldly figure of Haile Selassie, who had visited Jamaica in April 1966, met Rasta leaders, and paid his respects at Garvey's tomb. The emperor, for whom divine right to rule was also an issue, repeatedly used the concept of human rights as part of his denunciation of Africa's colonial regimes and the racism that secured them.

Bearing this history in mind, we must consider what there was about Marley's command of music and words which enabled the overdeveloped and underdeveloped worlds, the global North and South, to communicate in new ways and, through the media of his music and poetry, to discover elements of a common culture in which their differing concerns might come together. Rights were a significant part of this, but the idea of humanity is also implicated, particularly once it had pointedly

been redefined in opposition to the racism that made authentic, disalienated humanism impossible.

Marley was, among other things, a clever translator articulating the
disarmingly intelligent voices of the poor and the wretched in a tongue
that the more privileged could not fail to comprehend. The cosmopolitan pattern of his I-niversalism altered the fields of political force
around national states and national cultures. It showed where their borders had started to leak and how their ecologies of belonging were being
transformed as the Cold War, which had made Jamaica such a strategic
location, came to an end. This pattern would become much more elaborate with the consolidation of the new communications technology.

Marley's stardom also makes sense in the historical and cultural context provided by the demise of rock and roll. He was the last rock star,
and also the first figure of a new phase identified as the beginning of
what has come to be known as "world music," a significant marketing
category that helps to locate historically the slow, terminal demise of the
music-led youth culture which faded out with the embers of the twentieth century. The rise of world music certainly did mark a new phase
in the global struggle over cultural commodities and the terms of cultural production. But it also signalled rather more than the fact that the
whole world was available for the delectation of well-heeled consumers in the overdeveloped countries. Where world music ceased to be a
marketing label and became an ethically infused aspiration, it can also
help to identify a uniquely cosmopolitan space where musicians from
all sorts of places and backgrounds could begin—once again in opposition to the hierarchies of race and the logics of empire—to meet one
another as equals. In that utopian location, they could imagine what it
might mean to create together on the singular foundation of common
human creativity—in real time and face to face. Bob's legacy encouraged
that possibility and showed where sufferers could not only synchronise
the tempos of their dissent, as he had done with Britain's eager punks,
but also start to interact outside the marketing rules established by Bab-

ylon's cultural industries. The Alabaman guitarist Wayne Perkins was one of several white musicians involved in Marley's first international release. His account of how he came to add the bluesy guitar to "Baby We've Got a Date" and, most important, to "Concrete Jungle," the opening track of the Wailers' Island Records debut *Catch-a-Fire*, illustrates how a creative coming together made language secondary to the magical intimacy of real-time musical interaction.

> So I'm listening and I'm sitting there trying to figure out what's going on and I can't find the one, to save my ass I can't find the one! All of a sudden something starts to settle in. . . . They started playing this strange music I'd never heard the likes of. Compared to anything else I'd ever heard in my life, . . . this was backwards.
>
>   . . . And I had this pedal on at the end of the solo, as I recall, which was a sustain pedal from Manny's that I'd bought in New York. You hit this thing and it held the note forever—it would hold the note for three minutes. And as it held that one note, it would start to feed back an octave higher and then two octaves higher than that. When that happened . . . somebody hit the echo on that thing. It rang across the room. . . . It sent everybody. . . . It gave *me* goosebumps. It was one of those magic moments. Marley came running out there saying, "That's it, man," trying to pat me on the back and everything, . . . and I had no idea what he was saying.[49]

Away from the ludic pleasures of the recording studio, however, Marley's unbounded popularity was built upon the universal power of a language that was simultaneously and inextricably both poetic and political. Its original, biblical configurations had been created by slaves whose early claims on the New World's colonial modernity had been established when they were themselves reduced to the status of commodi-

ties for sale on a global market. This distinctive relationship to language
had been further shaped by a history of exile from literacy on pain of
death. Instead of their freedom, the slaves had been given only a King
James Bible with which to make the brutal world of the monocrop plantation intelligible. After its Caribbean rebirth, the tentacles of African
orature reached outward and eventually located distant audiences hungry for the commonsense wisdom and insight that were being offered by
the custodians of black Atlantic tradition. The notions of freedom that
Du Bois had identified as a gift to the world were eagerly received and
bent to new purposes.

Marley's music had been pirated into Eastern Europe long before the
Berlin Wall and the Iron Curtain fell. It became intertwined with the
longing for freedom and rights that was evident in every variety of regime—across Africa, the Pacific, and Latin America. Captured on cas-
settes and vinyl, that rebel music travelled far from its original sources
and discovered new constituencies, particularly among indigenous and
colonised people. Rebel reggae thrived across the planet. The Jamaican
style was heard, copied, and then blended into the local traditions of
Brazil, Surinam, Okinawa, Japan, Australia, New Zealand, and numerous African countries, particularly Zimbabwe, Zaïre, South Africa, and
Ivory Coast. It would be a huge mistake to imagine that this development
happened by accident or resulted from some natural, organic process.
This was cultural work. Nor should we overlook the grueling tours undertaken by Marley's hardworking band. Their eventual breakthrough
was founded as much on the demanding labour of transcontinental
market-building as on the visionary qualities Marley invested in the
language of sufferation that he made so compelling. In the years 1976–
1980, his final version of the Wailers road show criss-crossed the globe,
performing in the United States, the United Kingdom, Canada, France,
Italy, Germany, Spain, Scandinavia, Ireland, Holland, Belgium, Swit-
zerland, Japan, Australia, New Zealand, Ivory Coast, and Gabon. Significant sales were also recorded in areas where the band did not get to
perform, particularly Brazil, Senegal, Ghana, Nigeria, Taiwan, and the

Philippines. This global route suggests that Marley's ultimate success should be seen in a new context. It was the outcome of a larger process of cultural and political realignment and reconstruction whereby blackness ceased to be the primary cultural property of African Americans and became something else, which would operate primarily not on an East-West axis, but on the different geo-political architecture of North-South conflicts.

That lesson is underlined if we join the cosmopolitan history of these musical forms with another, even less fashionable history: that of the oppositional, anti-imperial political movements of the Cold War period.[50] There are a number of valuable points to be made. During the twentieth century, this music and the moral economy in which it had been enmeshed reached a point where they became not just dialogic or heterological expressions of interconnection, solidarity, and synchronised belonging but could plausibly be understood as planetary, cosmopolitan, and, loosely speaking, anti-imperialist resources. This may have been what Bob Marley intended when he described himself as a secret revolutionary.

The unprecedented reach of this new world music facilitated the translatability of the moral and political sentiments with which it was caught up. The resulting transcultures were unpredictable, chaotic, and lacking in fixed centres. Their planetary character illuminates a history of that century in which the dissenting cultures of the black Atlantic, forged in slavery and suffering and resting upon a distinctive critique of capitalism to which antislavery had given rise, contradicted the globalising pretensions of American imperial and commercial culture. This tension was played out repeatedly in the development of insurgent reggae music.

One brief example will have to suffice here. Michael Henderson, sometime fretless bass player with Miles Davis' early 1970s electric groups, left and developed a second chapter to his distinguished professional career as a baritone crooner of soul and disco material. His initial employer in this new role was the drummer Norman Connors.

The most memorable song that emerged from their collaboration was a slow romantic ballad released in 1977, "You Are My Starship." The song remains an unusual presence within the cold current of vernacular Afro-futurism. It attempted an update of the strategy initiated by Robert Johnson on "Terraplane Blues." This time, however, the liberatory vehicle with which the lover's serenaded body had merged was an interplanetary one. The lover's body was no longer *only* being compared to a vehicle. Here the receptive female body provided the singer with a means of escape to another world which was also another time. Loving tenderness became otherworldly. It afforded welcome relief from the tensions of a harsh environment defined by the operation of racial hierarchy. Against the historical backdrop provided by the mainstream popularity of *Star Wars* and *Close Encounters of the Third Kind,* this piece of domestic science fiction made sex into the favoured means of healing and repair.

> Yes, you are my starship,
> Come take me up tonight, and don't be late
> And don't you come too soon
> Baby, yeah.

Some years after the U.S. record had first reached Jamaica, it was covered in a reggae style by Freddie McGregor, another distinguished graduate from Coxsone's Studio One. Alongside his roots output, Freddie had built up a track record of reworking popular U.S. rhythm-and-blues songs like LTD's "Love Ballad." His 1980 version of the Connors-Henderson song involved a radical transformation that altered more than the rhythmic character of the original. The basic arrangement was retained, but the piece acquired a completely different lyric. McGregor also renamed the song "Natural Collie" and turned it into an anthemic defence of smoking herb, in line with the theology of the Twelve Tribes of Israel organisation to which he then belonged. Beyond its paean to the natural fruits of the earth, the song articulated a memorable cry of universal sufferation that—rarely for this idiom—linked the need to smoke herb to the healing properties of marijuana, which were seen as a necessary therapy, given the scale of people's everyday problems. Collie weed (ganja) was presented here as a natural, authentic substance endowed with welcome anaesthetic properties. Freddie McGregor's song celebrated its power on behalf of Jamaica's righteous poor: the sufferers who were internally exiled, locked out from the official world of Babylonian exploitation. Herb was the foundation of ritual countermemory. It was a sacrament, and, as such, it was a means by which they could acquire an uplifting, spiritual inspiration that might transcend their sufferings and point to higher freedoms than any bodily comfort could supply.

> People, look around you. Can't you see we're living in poverty.
> This pain is too much for me. Oh Jah, oh Jah, oh Jah.
> Save the people.
> Free them from captivity. This pain is too much to be.

The differences between these two versions of the song encapsulate how the vernacular culture of the late twentieth-century black Atlantic encompassed a confrontation between two incompatible cultural outlooks routed from slavery. The "northern" variant was basically comfortable with the idea that private, romantic passion could provide adequate compensation for public inequality, and enacted its aspirations within the categories of an oppressive system. The second, "southern" approach was utopian, though not placeless. It was energised by revolutionary hope and oriented by a critical worldliness. The split between these two stances did not, of course, coincide tidily with the border between the overdeveloped United States and its exploited Caribbean back yard, but the tensions between those locations helps to illuminate it further. The utopia being made audible in the second case was regularly specified in visionary fragments. Bunny Wailer's song "Dreamland" and the Isley Brothers' "Atlantis" both spring to mind, but there were plenty of other twinned allegories featuring Black Power on one side and, on the other, the hope of a future without racism in which race has been drained of meaning. Zion has triumphed against Babylon. The children of Israel have risen up against Egypt and departed for the Promised Land.

Though the privatisation and commodification of culture are also parts of the story that Marley's music helps us to re-tell, the protectionist impulses of today's would-be copyright holders and culture police have been more usually warranted under the signs of heritage and tradition than the banners of insatiable commerce. The authority of those imagined collectivities confirms that the reconciliation of culture and nationality with ethnic property and racial propriety has usually been achieved through specific articulations of space and place. This territorialisation has relied upon the idea that tight and unbreakable "sovereign" associations between a cultural form and its characteristic setting can be divined. Every cultural expression compliments an ecology to which it primarily belongs. Away from the interaction which distinguishes that place, its particular culture loses its unique coherence, and its power to command attention will be diminished.

For some time now, the national state has occupied a privileged position in the calculations of cultural worth promoted by these decidedly modern strategies. The political value and even the moral value of nationality have been critical in establishing the evasive criteria by which cultures can be compared, evaluated, and ranked. The post-traditional traditions of this black Atlantic music have introduced some attractive alternatives to that Germanic cultural axiology. They are at risk of being captured back into that disabling approach whenever their history gets conscripted into nation-building projects like the one which accorded Marley and Dennis Brown state funerals and made them into the cornerstones of national heritage. At its best, however, this music has voiced its own contrary conceptions of cultural value, specified its understanding of the place of culture in nonevolutionary, conflictual, but not dialectical progress, and nurtured mechanisms of accountability that have been folded back into the sociality of its production and its use by groups at varying distances from its point of origin.

These musical traditions do not always fit neatly into the stories of ethnic resilience, heroic masculinity, national liberation, racial ascent, and vindication that would serve the immediate political interests of its creators, whether they are African Americans defending, protesting, or affirming or postcolonial Caribbean nations seeking postcolonial stability and income from reggae tourism.

The integrity of national states and cultures remains a contested issue, not least in methodological terms, but it seems more productive to discuss shifting the interpretive settings that determine the scale upon which histories of twentieth-century black culture are to be written. This requires changing our understanding of culture and its workings so that the priority accorded to national states, national identity, and national solidarity is even less automatic and totalising. The claims of nationality can then be offset against the contending dynamics of locality, neighbourhood, region, and other subnational formations, as well as the bigger translocal connections, exchanges, and dialogues that have shaped these formations through outernational and antinational circuitry, giving them long-distance reach and other recombinant qualities that have made them ubiquitously attractive.

The Limits of Ethiopianism

All the basic facts of Bob Marley's life are well known. He was born in Nine Miles, Jamaica, on February 6, 1945. His Anglo-Jamaican father was a minor colonial functionary who had tried his luck in several different British imperial outposts before winding up in the Caribbean. His mother was a young black peasant woman thirty-two years her husband's junior. Marley's long-ignored father does not appear to have been involved in the boy's upbringing. However, the absent paternal figure has been brought forward and offered as a key to interpreting his son's extraordinary achievements and comprehending the unusual motivation to succeed that took the boy out of the Trenchtown settlement where he passed his teenage years. This in turn raises the pathology of mixedness which often functions as the ironic counterpoint to Bob's visionary creativity. It also suggests that the period in which he could be represented as primitive, exotic, and dangerous was drawn to a close some time ago. Instead, we can observe a prodigal, almost child-like Marley being brought home into the bosom of the corporate family where the imposing figure of Chris Blackwell—the white Jamaican producer and entrepreneur who oversaw the Wailers' greatest commercial successes—stands in for the biological father that Bob never knew. Blackwell seems to believe that he exercised a variety of parental authority over Marley, which guided his compromises and scripted his tactical bargains with the music business.

Marley had endured a difficult childhood as what might now be called a "mixed-race" or "biracial" child. It introduced him not only to poverty and to the viciousness of racial hierarchies, but also to the antipathy and suspicion that can be directed from both sides of the colour line at people whose bodies carry the unsettling evidence of transgressive intimacy between black and white. This personal history is increasingly being introduced as a primary explanation of Marley's character, drive, and ambition. It is even suggested that his being a "half-caste" can help to account for the ways he was able to pursue and articulate cultural identity, and may also explain the power with which he encountered and projected blackness not only as a politics but also as what the Rastafari call "livity" (a whole way of life). Whether his unusual formation was so mechanistically and obviously at the root of Bob's artistic and philosophical visions is hard to say. It would be foolish to deny those unusual early experiences any significance, but how they register in what followed needs to be carefully considered.

Marley's life suggests that the conventional understanding of this problem should be provocatively reversed. Contrary to the stereotype, simply having "mixed" parentage seems not to have been a handicap for him, but rather to have conferred some interpretive advantages and stimulated him towards useful insights into the character and limits of both identity and groupness. In his approach to the former, solidarity trumped the power of sameness. In his consideration of the latter, the appeal of racial seriality is undone by the history of bitter strife inside the collective. He requires us to reflect upon whether the differences that appear between racial groups are of a completely different variety from the divisions and hierarchies that erupt within them. How do those two varieties of conflict become connected when colonial governments operate according to the strategic imperatives of divide and rule? What answers does the mixed-race person give to the apostles of purity, who can be found in all communities?

Marley's obvious appetite for these questions, to which he offers more than merely political answers, shows that his background had become useful to him. It appears also to have been the first of a number of atypical experiences that endowed his poetic work with a rare depth, and infused his commitment to music with a tenacity that drew additional power from a long creative association with his childhood friends Bunny Livingstone and Peter Tosh. In their talented and resourceful company, the choice of a musical career became more than a romantic alternative to life as an apprentice welder. Marley did not look forward to the prospect of fulfilling himself in a life of drudgery.

It is clear that, before he was able to rationalise his distaste for Babylon via the biblical poetry of the burgeoning Rastafari movement, Marley was a stylish and rebellious youth, despite his poverty. Though mostly raised in a rural environment, he was drawn to the dynamic urban figure of the "rude boy." Like many teenagers elsewhere during the 1950s, Jamaican youth were turning towards more immediate forms of gratification, pleasure, and play in a longer transition from child to adult and a greater degree of economic autonomy. Youth itself was emerging as a state in which authority would be questioned, and the allegiance of young people to the order that their elders had established or accepted could not be taken for granted. This outlook was fed by the mythography of imported African American rhythm and blues.

Marley and his friends launched their musical adventure in 1963. They had been captivated by the sound and promise of black American music that had been produced during an unusually rich and creative period in its history. In a 1973 interview, both Marley and Tosh told the British music magazine *Melody Maker* that Curtis Mayfield was their favourite songwriter and performer.[51] Black America's explosion of music making was associated with the accelerated modernisation process that attended the northward migration of rural people who were still close to and deeply scarred by the experience of slavery.[52] The electrification of their blues, the secularisation and profanation of their church-based musical forms, and the special qualities that arose from that no-longer-sacred music's proximity to righteous demands for civil and political rights spoke to remote audiences far from where their culture had been initially brought to life.[53] These profound changes enriched the cultural world of desperate young whites in the United States and in Europe with a new and exhilarating soundscape. They reached into the everyday lives of far-flung black populations to whom African American freedom discourse offered a way to understand their own experiences of marginality and frustration.

Jamaica was no exception to these new cultural rules. Clustered around a radio that brought them access to Miami stations WINZ and WGBS, Bob, Bunny, Peter, and their musical associates were able to listen in to the dynamic soundtrack of this extraordinary period of conflict and transition in American society. The rhythm-and-blues sounds of artists like Louis Jordan, Amos Milburn, Calvin Boze, and eventually Ray Charles had nurtured the competitive DJ culture around Jamaica's sound systems (groups of DJs who set up turntables and speakers on the streets to play ska and reggae) and the "rude boy" outlook of the teens who supported them. The wildest and hippest records were being shipped in from the United States by sound-system operators like Duke Reid and Coxsone Dodd. These entrepreneurs would be the first to record and promote the music made by local artists. It was Dodd who gave the Wailers their first break at Studio One.

The harmony singing of U.S. groups like the Coasters and the Drifters proved extremely popular in the Caribbean, providing inspiration to local musicians whose own art started to evolve in a dense and complex dialogue with diverse North American styles, from jazz to country and western. The eventual recipe for the Wailers' own revolutionary musical output would combine local flavours with the delicate militancy of Curtis Mayfield's glorious recordings with the Impressions and the Clavinet-driven "street funk" of later U.S. groups like Mandrill, War, and the Meters.

Under the direction of their early mentor, Joe Higgs, they took Mayfield's secular seriousness, and approximated the smooth, sweet vocal arrangements that blended his exquisite falsetto voice with those of Sam Gooden and Fred Cash. This version of soft soul music dominated the Wailers' output until Mayfield became a solo artist and turned his own output towards a funkier stream of social commentary combined with innovative, textured musical soundscapes. James Brown had brought the political language of Black Power into the centre of the dance floor, and Sly and the Family Stone refined its rhythmic signatures. After those shifts, the Wailers would urge their own backing musicians—who were already adept at approximating the U.S. sound—to introduce the stuttering syncopations of bass-heavy New Orleans' second-line funk into the more even textures of local beats like rocksteady and ska. Rebel reggae was the exhilarating result of this exercise in cross-fertilisation. Once again, hybridity, mixture, and contaminating combination can be seen as sources of excitement and strength, rather than symptoms of weakness and pathology.

At that time, many Jamaican emigrants found the traditional imperial pathway to Britain blocked by their country's 1962 acquisition of independence. Barred from relatively easy entry into England by the introduction of stricter governmental controls,[54] Marley was one of many who sought another route towards self-reliance and economic opportunity by moving to the United States. During his early twenties, he followed his mother, Cedella Booker, to Wilmington, Delaware, where she had married a U.S. citizen. Bob settled on the East Coast for a while, determined to explore the segregated and turbulent world that he had apprehended and learned to love from the songs of the black troubadours who inspired him.[55]

According to his mother's account of this period, Marley fared badly as a would-be docker and "eventually, after some trying, [he] got a job as a janitor at the Dupont Hotel and settled down to work his daily shift and save his money."[56] The first of his two substantial spells in the United States lasted for eight months, during 1966. This was after the triumphs of the civil rights movement, which had come with the passing of landmark legislation—the Civil Rights Act (1964) and the Voting Rights Act (1965)—by the Johnson administration. Those big political victories were epochal, but they were also deceptive. This was still a time of great conflict and bitterness in American society.

Many commentators have seen this particular period as critical. It hosted an important transition. The next phase in the freedom struggle would not be dominated by a nonviolent civil rights movement. The very different moods which expressed the Black Power ideology emerged after the murder of Malcolm X in February 1965. The Black Panther party was founded in Oakland, California, in October of the following year. From this point on, community defence was to be accomplished by any means necessary, and the struggles of African Americans became closely identified with the wars being fought elsewhere for national liberation from colonial rule. Black America's new, younger leadership likened U.S. ghettos to colonies and the militancy of organisations like the Black Panthers suggested that their fight against segregationism and white supremacy would be conducted in the same spirit as an anticolonial war.

During June of that first year in Wilmington, the famous civil rights activist James Meredith was ambushed and shot in broad daylight during his "Walk against Fear" from Memphis, Tennessee, to Jackson, Mississippi. The same fateful period saw the U.S. civil rights movement extend its hopes and ambitions out of the rural South and into the wretched urban spaces of the northern states, where racism assumed more subtle and less obvious forms. There, the opposition to racial terror and white supremacy shifted towards a more open-ended battle against economic inequality, segregated dwelling, and political disenfranchisement. Martin Luther King's opposition to the war in Vietnam and Malcolm X's shift away from simple nationalism were important indicators of this new phase.

The move away from nonviolence and towards legitimate force deployed in self-defence was registered in Marley's imagination. That change was starkly dramatised in the narrative of "I Shot the Sheriff," which, in a telling way, used an American setting to stage a parable of resistance against injustice that could have taken place anywhere. There are no sheriffs or deputies in Jamaica, but there was extensive rioting in Atlanta, Detroit, Philadelphia, and other major U.S. cities during Marley's first summer. It seems clear that the desperate scenario which would be affirmed years later in the mournful, resigned phrases of his most haunting song, "Burnin' and Lootin'," was imprinted in his consciousness at this time. He returned to Jamaica after eight months, carrying a collection of electronic equipment to be used in the next stage of his musical career.

We must pause over this part of his life to consider the portrait of him that it suggests—namely, as an exploited, grumbling, and deeply disaffected immigrant worker in U.S. heavy industry and traditional service work. The 1966 spell in Delaware was the first of several visits to black America: a nation-within-a-nation that was changing its sense of itself under the internal impact of Black Power ideology, riot, and protest. That community was also being altered fundamentally by popular opposition to the war in Indochina, protests in which the leaders of the black movement were becoming increasingly prominent and vocal, attracting the surveillance and then the hostility of the U.S. government, which set out to undermine and disrupt their activities. The special power of music in these new circumstances must have been evident to Marley as he followed the career of Curtis Mayfield out of the more innocent era characterised by "Gypsy Woman" and "People Get Ready" and into the militant and affirmative statements he made on records like "We're a Winner" and "A Choice of Colors."

Once again, the characteristic pattern revealed in Marley's life was one of cultural fusion and intermixture. He was inspired by the moral energy and political acumen of African American performers who embraced the mission given to them by civil rights and Black Power. He saw that a similar commitment could be fused with older Jamaican traditions, which usefully blurred the line between cultural, ethical, spiritual, and political action. But further formative experiences outside of Jamaica were necessary before that combination could gel. Marley learned and grew through commercial and musical associations with several African Americans. Among them was Johnny Nash, the Texan actor and singer who crossed-over Marley-penned songs into the British pop chart. Nash brought Marley to Europe, and 1971 found them lodging in Sweden, where Bob had encountered some of the white southern American musicians who would later embellish his historic Island recordings with rock motifs, so that the music could appeal to bigger, broader audiences. Itinerancy stimulated Marley in other ways too. The enigmatic songs "Kinky Reggae" and "Midnight Ravers" reveal his perplexity in the face of the wild urban scene he found in London. Most, though not all, of his hostility and suspicion is adapted into a more relaxed and amused sense of the endless permutations of blackness.

That possibility even released a surreal glimpse of Garvey as a flâneur in the swirl of the city's cosmopolitan excess:

> I went down to Piccadilly circus and down there I saw Marcus
> He had a candy tar all over his chocolate bar

This nomadic pattern suggests that travel rather than rootedness, and itinerant rather than sedentary cultural habits, guided Bob towards a new sense of what music could accomplish.

Like many young Jamaicans of the generation that had witnessed their country's independence and applauded its uncoupling from British colonial rule, Marley had been drawn towards the Rastafari culture of Jamaica's popular Ethiopianist movement. The 1960s and '70s saw that current of feeling being reinvigorated by the fallout from U.S. Black Power and by the struggles against European domination of colonial countries like Mozambique, Guinea Bissau, Rhodesia, and of course South Africa.

Traditional Ethiopianism, which had been politicised in 1938,[57] was able to combine a strong spiritual and poetic aspect with an elaborate critique of exploitation and a principled hostility to the habitual injustices of colonial law. It gave expression to a militant indictment of the routine horrors of colonial rule, which were still very much in evidence after Jamaica's formal independence from Britain had been achieved. Its imaginative horizons were now expanded to include the colonial dimensions of black struggle. The CIA and the Monroe doctrine were reaching into Jamaican political culture. As black politics became Cold War geo-politics, the idea of return to the African source from which the journey into slavery had commenced was complicated by a novel sense of solidarity, kinship, and translocal identification. After all, Jamaica was close to Cuba and the Cubans were assisting the African freedom struggle.[58]

Guided by the precepts of race first and self-reliance that had been established earlier in the twentieth century by Marcus Garvey, the Rastafari of Jamaica focused their attention upon the independent African state of Ethiopia, which was seen as a vehicle for worldwide black emancipation. Marley was in the United States and missed Selassie's visit to the island. The emperor's presence brought the world into colonial Jamaica, but it was Marley who would give postcolonial Jamaica a voice in the world. His growing interest in Rastafari began to contribute a powerful mystical dimension to his poetry. The chorus of "Trenchtown Rock" provocatively and ironically introduced the brutality of music into a joyful song intended to heal the inhuman effects of brutality. What had primarily been a moral and economic antipathy against the injustices of colonial rule became, for an instant, more straightforwardly political. The Rastafari insistence upon the fundamental significance of history strengthened Marley's sense of the divided world beyond the Caribbean. Their alternative history operated on the cosmopolitan scale he would later employ to describe Zimbabwe's war of independence as a "little struggle" and to compile his inventory of the multiple varieties of trouble in the world. The Rastafari could fluently explain the four-hundred-year saga of racial capitalism. They used their familiarity with that grim tale to explain why selfishness and disengagement were unacceptable.

Antipolitical Politics and the Cry of Love

The trans-local platform Marley occupied as the first truly global pop star was created not only by the protest music of Bob Dylan and the Beatles but by the achievements of African American athletes like Jack Johnson, Jesse Owens, Joe Louis, and Muhammad Ali. Their heroic physicality was appreciated everywhere for the insubordinate answer it gave to white supremacy and for the larger human story of triumph-over-adversity which could be read from it. The power of their stories was increased during the aftermath of Fascism, when Europe sought a cultural renewal and discovered it in the accomplishments of African American musicians, artists, and writers. What was called "youth culture" derived from this apprehension which was captured by Aimé Césaire's observation that postwar Europe was a decaying civilisation incapable of solving the historical problems to which it had given rise: the colonial problem and the problem of the proletariat.[59] Its young people would acquire resources for renewal from some unlikely places. First rock and roll and then jazz, soul, and reggae provided stimuli for the unfolding of a new pattern of subculture in which class, gender, and generational relations would be actively recomposed along more egalitarian lines. A new relationship to the world of blackness and a new politics of race were forged in this moment, and they persisted throughout the postwar years.

It matters little that Marley's translocal appeal was built upon a number of political, technological, and historical contingencies that have little to do either with the quality of his art or with the dimensions of his revolutionary political theology. The end of the Cold War, the emergence of new markets for pop culture in the developing world, the rise of green thinking, and related issues like the exhaustion of socialism, and the redundancy of the vision of utopia which had arisen from the idea that industrial development could be harnessed for the greater good, were all factors that contributed to his appeal.

But there was another important element that usually gets overlooked. The end of European empires had settled large numbers of colonial subjects inside the citadels of overdevelopment. Jamaicans and other Caribbean folk had been drawn into English society as a replacement population quite prepared to undertake the dirty, dangerous, and poorly paid jobs that white workers no longer wanted. As the years went by, the original citizen settlers had reproduced and created a new generation of black subjects who knew no other homes than the concrete jungles of the postindustrial cities. These young European citizens were equipped with a sense of entitlement that their parents had not been able to enjoy. They were not prepared to accept the racism and hostility that the previous generation had borne stoically and patiently. This young population did not recognise itself in the marginal category "second-generation immigrant." Its demand for substantive rather than merely formal citizenship was as firm and articulate as its opposition to racism was absolute. These young people wanted a culture that would correspond to their embattled predicament. Marley was one of the great Jamaican artists who gave it to them, and it was this group which provided the backbone of the Wailers' international audience. The worldwide dissemination of Black Power and Rastafari cultures furnished them with raw materials from which a new version of black identity would be artfully assembled.

In Britain, various groups of young people, some white, some black, would be invited to the punky reggae party. They were divided by racism, but connected by their youth and their distaste for injustice, authoritarianism, and militarism. With their support, Marley became not only the first truly global pop icon, but a historic figure whose revolutionary art connected the old modern culture of slaves and slave descendants with the very different political tempo of the postcolonial world.

By linking the freedom struggles and pursuit of human rights and dignity by Western Hemisphere blacks to the national liberation movements of Africa, Bob Marley represents more than the transition of the Atlantic diaspora's Ethiopianist imagination into a more worldly or perhaps more thoroughly cosmopolitan mode. Along with many other reggae performers who shared his beliefs, he made the history and memory of racial slavery into an interpretive device that could be turned towards innumerable varieties of injustice and unfreedom.

The political tradition from which he sprang has a number of features that made it attractive to youthful rebels and expand the conception of politics which is at stake here. The sanctification of ganja no doubt helped to win their attention, as well as to clarify the important difference between unjust laws made by governments and the higher, natural forms of law that governed the interaction between the Rastafari and their environment. There is another attribute of this outlook that is worth identifying. The Rasta view approaches work in a specific way and does not identify it either with self-mastery or with happiness. Waged work should be seen, instead, in relation to the history of slavery. This comparison reveals work to be essentially coercive: an alienating, dis-spiriting obligation that crushes the life and humanity out of people, leaving them nothing of themselves to use on more rewarding, humane, and creative pursuits. The work ethic on which capitalism and Babylon rely is overthrown by alternatives we can describe as the play ethic or the love ethic, in which the highest value is placed on nonwork time, friendship, intimacy, and care. These are the values affirmed in Mar-ley's best-known song, "No Woman, No Cry." A caring masculinity gets linked there with a quiet defence of communal living and a muted cri-tique of private property, delivered tenderly from the depths of proper-tylessness.

Among the Rastafari and their followers, the ritualised, public ma-nipulation of language was appreciated as a major source of pleasure and given the special name "reasoning." That form of self-creation is valued more highly than the work of imprinting oneself and one's own industry upon nature. This stance rejects the idea that industrialisation can be identified with human progress and looks for deeper experiences of human being in the world than those which are most highly prized by the unjust arrangements that Peter Tosh described as the "general shit-stem" (system).

Until Marley, being against that modernity had necessitated the quest for a place beyond or outside it. The alternative, utopian location was identified with a return to Africa; but after his intervention, the idea of a permanent, physical return was no longer uppermost. He made it pos-sible to imagine and to practice other kinds of solidarity and to appreci-ate the in-between positions and experiences that arose in transit be-tween nodal points on a new, cosmopolitan network.

Marley's transnational appeal and espousal of itinerant culture in-vite speculation about the status of identity and the conflicting scales on which sameness, subjectivity, and solidarity could be conceived. Connecting with his legacy across the webs of planetary popular culture might even be thought of as an additional stage in the nonprogressive evolution of the African diaspora into the digital era. Recognising this possibility requires moving the focus of our inquiry away from the notions of fixed or closed identity that we have already discovered to be worn out. Attention should be placed instead upon the processes and mechanisms of identification. Do people connect themselves and their hopes with the mythic figure of Bob Marley as a man, a Jamaican, a Caribbean, an African, or a pan-African artist? He was somehow all of the above and yet more, a rebel voice of the poor and the underdeveloped world that made itself audible in the core of the overdeveloped social and economic life he called Babylon.

That complexity requires us to ask: What variety of cultural analysis can make sense of his reconciliation of modern and postmodern technologies with mystical and apparently antimodern forces? How do we combine his work as an organic intellectual, as a thinker and political actor, with his portrayal as a primitive, hypermasculine figure: a not-so-noble savage shrouded in clouds of sacred smoke? Are we prepared now, so many years after his death and canonisation, to set aside the new forms of minstrelsy obviously promoted under the constellation of his stardom and see him instead as a worldly figure whose career traversed continents and whose revolutionary political outlook won adherents because of its ability to imagine the end of capitalism as readily as it imagined the end of the world?

Marley's life and work continually overflowed from national structures. National states, national cultures, national movements are all inadequate if we are to interpret a life and a career that lend themselves to the study of diaspora identification that unfolds between the axes represented by geography on the one hand and genealogy on the other.

Moving away from those options, or, more accurately, shifting productively between them, can help us to perceive the workings of a complex cultural circuitry that has transformed a pattern of diaspora culture from a simple one-way dispersal, starting at a fixed point of origin, into a multinodal, webbed, or relational assemblage that is constituted through multiple points of intersection.

A sense of belonging uncomfortably to more than one place defines this decentred consciousness and imposes particular rules on the processes of self-making and self-love that can answer and perhaps reverse the damage done by racism. More than any other event, Bob's historic performance at the Zimbabwe independence ceremony in April 1980 symbolised a partial reconnection of the Atlantic diaspora with its African beginnings. Yet Bob did not opt to make Africa his home. Instead, as many other prominent Pan-Africanists have done before and since, he chose a more difficult and more cosmopolitan commitment that did not require his physical presence there.

This was a new stage in the life of the African diaspora into the Western Hemisphere, because it did not anticipate a return to the place of imaginary origin. With Marley and his peers, diaspora identity seems to have taken on its own life and to have cultivated its own forms of blackness, which were not African, or, more accurately, not *just* African. These complex attachments and transcultural habits have matured and assumed an independent life beyond Africa, which is no longer the receptacle of their worldly history. The challenge that results would be to make a new Pan-Africanism capable of operating beyond earlier concerns with return and solidarity.

Rather than fixing Africa in the frozen time of the prediasporic past, this emergent option would allow it into the present and the future. The memory of slavery and the history of race hierarchy would remain extremely important, but this diasporic consciousness could not be confined by or responsible for them. If this can be accomplished in Marley's memory, he will be commemorated as a world figure whose willingness to dream forwards revealed his unfashionable attachment to the idea of a better world.

There are two conventional approaches to understanding Marley's political imagination. Both of them are unsatisfactory. The first reduces him mechanically to his revolutionary political opinions. He becomes their sexy embodiment and little else. This view is a comforting one, because it suggests that the flames of resistance are inextinguishable and that they cannot be contained by governments, technologies, or the various cultural forces that promote selfishness and privatised experience.

The second view of Marley pretends that he had no substantive political or philosophical outlook. Those things are understood as decoration. This second diagnosis prefers to consider him instead as an exotic figure who was driven, according to the oldest logic of racial science, by feelings and instincts rather than by any intellect. Marley would be to the late twentieth century what Frederick Douglass was a hundred years earlier: the ideal masculine representation of his whole racial group. This is how he becomes the patron saint of soccer, ganja, Rasta, and machismo, a handsome presence on the coffee tables of the overdeveloped countries, where poverty can appear exotic against the backdrop of a tropical paradise and the idea of helping the natives and savages creates dubious feelings of charity among their racial and moral superiors.

It is time for these inadequate approaches to be given up. We need a more complex and radically historical portrait of Marley, his travels, and his accomplishments in various spheres. As yet, this emerges only fitfully and reveals the orthodox interpretations of his life to be shallow and trivial. His evolving politics, for example, must be understood with care. His consciousness of change shouldn't be reduced, on one side, to the routine insubordination that follows from the conflicts with the police over using herb, or, on the other, confined inside national borders by Marley's failed attempt to bring Jamaica's divided and militarised political system together, uniting the country's warring factions in the name of obligations (nation, nature, peace) that were higher than loyalty to party machines.

Of course, to the Rastafari, formal or official politics would always be dismissed as either "politricks" or "poly ticks," a larger number of bloodsuckers. If any politician grants you a favour, your indebtedness to them will allow them to control and manipulate you. But the Rastafari practice of wordplay meant that ritual denials of politics did not always mean what they seemed to say. The need for politics was proclaimed in the very same breath in which actually existing politics was denounced. This antipolitics was a critique of the inhospitable politics that confronts us still. Hostility to the politics we already know and have learned to despise was articulated implicitly in the name of a revolutionary outlook. This was defined precisely through its disavowal of the politics we have inherited and which we reject because it offers only repeated unfreedom and yet deeper injustice.

Marley's vernacular art identified and worked through the injurious effects of racism. He chronicled the destructive attachment to Christianity among blacks, the systematic hypocrisy of church, state, and government, the capricious brutality of police, and the violence of miseducation. His best songs combine a subtle indictment of the damage done to the poor and the oppressed by imperialism, capitalism, and exploitation with a strong and liberating sense of the damage that the poor and oppressed can do to each other in a situation where "all they want us to do is keep on killing one another."

This sense of complicity was how, perhaps unexpectedly, he started to transcend the narrowness of all race-based identity in favour of a broader, humanistic outlook that followed the simpler antiracist logic pronounced by Selassie in the famous speech that Marley set to music under the title "War." We can repeat it here: "Until the colour of a man's skin is of no more significance than the colour of his eyes, there will be war."

This position enlisted the future into the struggle against racial divisions. It made race and racism part of the past and prehistory of humanity. The universality of Marley's language of sufferation began with this transcendental commitment to an alternative order, but that is not where it ends. One key to its extraordinary appeal may reside in the frequency with which that incendiary word "human" crops up in Marley's sage diagnosis of the ills of Babylon. This word was a staple component of the Cold War liberalism of the mid twentieth century. The poetics of Rastafari blasted it out of its UNESCO context and started to make it serve futuristic purposes. Their appeal to the idea of the human made it take on new life, especially when it was brought into the orbit of antiracist and anti-imperialist thought. Then, the alienated humanity that was associated with racial divisions could be replaced by a nonracial alternative that suffers, loves, acts, and exercises its will, in reshaping the broken world we have inherited.

That world cannot be repaired, and we must learn to suffer the consequences of its fractured condition, but we always enjoy more power to reshape it than we usually allow ourselves to believe. Another world is possible, and Marley serenades its becoming. He offered a new theory and practice of revolutionary agency that accentuated the political will and responsibility of individuals, once they had been exposed to truth and stripped of the illusions that support the injustices of the present, in which *we* go hungry while *their* bellies are full. Truth and right were inseparable. Illusions must be burned.

An irreducible antagonism between them and us found expression in the antihumanist language of class conflict. It seems to sharpen the divisions that Selassie's eyes and skin—a nonracial humanism—would abolish. The novel patterns of cultural globalisation revealed by Marley's life return us to the immediacy of that visceral battle, but there are other dynamics of conflict, care, and restoration that are articulated together with it. In a *Melody Maker* interview from 1973, Marley disclosed that his own personal favourite musical recording was the Beatles' song "All You Need Is Love."[60] Perhaps the political force of his avowedly antipolitical outlook can be understood best if we focus on the value that he placed upon love. That emphasis chimes with the way that love emerged in the political language of other black radicals during the Cold

War period. Frantz Fanon, the militant psychiatrist from the Caribbean island of Martinique who took up the cause of the Algerian rebels, speaks of the need to trace love's perversities and imperfections if racism is going to be overthrown.[61] As is better known, Dr. Martin Luther King wrote at length about how African Americans could find the strength to cultivate the forms of love that would be necessary in order to maintain the ethical core of nonviolence in the face of persecution and provocation.[62]

Marley's revolutionary attachment to love belongs in that company. The love he exalts is romantic and sexual, but it is also playful, boastful, narcissistic, and communal. It is fundamentally a love of life itself, deeply imprinted by the memory of slavery as the suspended sentence of death which could be carried out at any time by masters and mistresses who act with impunity. This defence of life was tied to Marley's opposition to all war and to his stalwart advocacy of peace. This is his gift to us and to the future.

3

Troubadours, Warriors, and Diplomats

I am of no particular race. I am of the human race, a man at large in the human world, preparing a new race. I am of no specific region. I am of earth.   —Jean Toomer (1931)

In his extraordinary little book *The Negro and His Music* (1936), the Bahá'ì sage Alain Locke described the modern black peoples of the Americas as the "songsters of the western world." The Negro, he noted, had gradually become "America's troubadour." More than seven decades later, though we can argue over when the curtain might have fallen, we should agree that the era in which these assertions were unproblematic and straightforwardly convincing has drawn to a close. Locke's choice of a medieval word to express that special role was poignant at the time. And troubadours are an even more anachronistic presence these days. The entertainment in which they traded was bound to conventions lost long ago. The Negro monopoly on popular song has expired. Even during the 1930s, Locke had noted that their special role was becoming circumscribed and perhaps compromised by other factors: "One of the handicaps of Negro music today is that it is too popular. It is tarnished with commercialism and the dust of the marketplace."[1]

Locke's hopeful observations had been oriented by a Germanic view of how folk cultures could be elevated into the higher, classical forms which corresponded to the ideal configurations of nationhood. The rise of digital technology and the demise of the phonograph, which was the principal vehicle for so many communicative possibilities, marked the end of the special period that his words summon up. To note these changes involves more than a roundabout way of saying that the fundamental link between music and black Atlantic life is no longer what it was.

The cultural role and social significance of music making have been transformed several times since African American folk cultures were rapidly adapted to an unevenly electrified world. They were radically changed a second time by digitisation. It is hard but necessary to face the blunt consequences of that deep historical shift, which exceeded the impact of all technological innovations. The counter-cultural voice of black Atlantic popular music has faded out. Song and dance have lost their preeminent positions in the ritual and interpretive processes that both grounded and bounded communal life. If any oppositional spirit endures, it is a residual trace of what that historic formation accomplished when music was more central to the everyday lives of people, when it could articulate protest and dissent and, in particular, testify to the ability of the young to imagine better alternatives to a hopeless, broken world. In that period, music intimated utopian possibilities charged with political and moral radicalism, social responsibility, and an abiding love of freedom that had grown from the pressures of the slave past and then been preserved as an interpretive resource which could build resilience and help to make sense of the present.

The case of Bob Marley has enabled us to sketch the final phase of these developments. Yet the detailed history of the special period in which black Atlantic music—jazz, blues, soul, reggae, samba, salsa— turned into a planetary force remains to be written. First phonograph technology and then electricity amplified its anticipatory, antiphonic communitarianism. Instead of the transnational synthesis which we urgently need, we have a range of different kinds of historical studies. That expanding archive focuses attention on discrete problems like the music's corporate and commercial accommodations, on its deployment as part of the cultural Cold War,[2] and, most consistently, on the difficult and damaged lives of its most innovative and creative producers. Memories of this musical culture's brief but incontrovertible moral authority are hard to recover, but they remain accessible. They are haunting now as we watch its trivialisation and transformation into little more than a background accompaniment to the perils and pleasures of a new imperium.

I feel obliged to confess that my critical standpoint has been shaped by an acute sense of being bereft of responsible troubadours—a feeling that is a wider generational affliction. I do not wish to capitulate to the pressures which dictate a nostalgic relationship to the latter part of that departed golden age. And yet, at the same time, I can recall the glorious parade of black Atlantic performers that flowed through London's musical scenes between 1969, when I first started going out to enjoy live music, and the more recent point, when deskilling, aesthetic stagnation, and what can politely be called "recycling" all intervened to make live performances less alive and less pleasurable than they had been before.

I cannot avoid the sense of loss that results from having lived through that rare period. Responding to black culture's changes of moral tone and social orientation involves grieving for a certain fragile, precious relationship between music and political ethics in which the former amended, stretched, and enriched the latter. This acknowledgement encompasses a yearning for a certain quality of engagement and profundity previously evident in the music itself. Additional sadness is prompted by recollections of an aspiration towards ontological depth which has largely vanished both from vernacular musical performances and from the poetics that dramatises them. The signature quality of these losses might be defined by the depleted vitality of music that was mostly made and heard in real time.

My sadness at these changes is also connected to a desire for the restoration of a public culture in which art and social life, those different dimensions of our complex practice as a collectivity, could dissolve easily and pleasurably into each other. These sentimental reactions are compounded by a hankering for the time when some barrier might still have been evident between the spheres of entertainment and advertising. That was also a time when the antiphonic dialogue between voice and guitar, refined by the likes of Chuck Berry and Albert King, Buddy Guy and Albert Collins, was still a reliable indicator of the well-being of something more than just the health of the individuals who gave exciting expression to it. In that fragile moment, it was still fruitful to ask—in settings provided by a dynamic, oppositional mood—the fateful and heroic existential question that Ralph Ellison had previously identified in Louis Armstrong's epic performance: "What did I do to be so black and so blue?"

That question was beginning to be asked transnationally and almost placelessly, as well as regionally. It was raised in ways that anticipated answers at the level of abstraction which had been defined for me as a black teenager in Cold War Europe by the small but promising window through which James Brown, in the guise of the "New Minister of the Super Heavy Funk," had observed the joyous activities of "the long-haired hippies and the Afro-blacks" dancing on the goodfoot. JB's profane vantage point was adjacent to another historic location, from which Sly Stone had surveyed the political and psychological debris of the 1960s and made his alternative "Sex Machine" a disturbing piece of music without words—a piece directed towards the awareness that words would never, could never, be enough to tell the misanthropic race-transcending stories that were apparently driving him out of his mind: "Don't call me nigger, whitey. Don't call me whitey, nigger."

The emergent global audiences for African American culture were

a long way from Chocolate City and sweet home Chicago, but they too
could discover themselves in the traveling truths of the people who were
now even darker than an Ellisonian shade of blue. In London, we needed
that remote input because elements of their transatlantically trouba-
doured analysis corresponded to our beleaguered predicament. We read
the literature of African American freedom culture and adapted its advocacy of civil rights to our different, immediately and obviously postcolonial situation. The world listened carefully to the vernacular trans-
missions pulsing from Black Power's cultural crucible.

Extraordinary things can still be heard in the enduring music of that
uniquely soulful era. The live recordings made by Aretha, Curtis Mayfield, and Donny Hathaway have proved particularly durable. As they
established new aesthetic criteria for African American popular music,
they seemed to invite even their most distant listeners into a collective
that felt intimate in spite of its attenuated, outernational character. Eager crowds had been dynamic collaborators in those epoch-making
performances. Perhaps that surprising possibility should be recalled,
now that the art of live recording has shrunk to fit the hyper-real,
pseudo-classical niche in which we are told authentic jazz performances
still dwell.

Curtis Mayfield's concert recordings captured the kernel of this
magic. After his shamanic January 1972 shows at the Rainbow Theatre in
London's Finsbury Park, an imaginary line linking him to James Brown
(then becoming known as the Godfather) constituted one axis of my
own nascent, "uk blak" mindset. The contemporary contrast between
Kanye West's ironic appetite for branded finery and 50 Cent's scarred,
muscular, Republican frame prompts us to ask: Where can Mayfield's
dignity and bespectacled seriousness have gone? Not, surely, into the
global business enterprise that has been built up so skillfully by brand
Jay Zee?

Curtis' example worked its wonders in other places too. In Jamaica,
Bunny Wailer was one of many singers who copied his falsetto phrasing;
and, as we have seen, Bob Marley was inspired by his political courage

and imagination. Curtis had bravely raised and reworked the issue of black America's roots long before Alex Haley took that limelight. If the Wailing Wailers built their early work on the templates provided by old Impressions tunes like "People Get Ready" and "Minstrel and Queen," they also appropriated Curtis' timeliness and his clear-sighted orientation towards peace and war, as well as the disabling features of contemporary capitalism that he would struggle to name on his later, solo records like "Future Shock," "Back to the World," and "There's No Place Like America Today."

I am inclined to overlook many problems in the romantic workings of the insurgent, prefeminist culture found on recordings like "I'm So Proud" and "Woman's Got Soul." Some of their more dubious qualities now sound like strengths when compared to the unmemorable, misogynistic, and fraternalist forms that succeeded them, simulating community for commercial ends rather than enacting it in the people's cause.

Extensive debate surrounds the periodisation of twentieth-century black American music. That problem is skirted here and reduced to an account of the regression from modernist conjuring with culture to postmodernist iconising and muting it. Instead, I want to centre my critical consideration of these musical affirmations of freedom, peace, and hope on the themes of memory and remembrance. The moral economy of the black Atlantic freedom movement did not prove easy to erase. A recursive operation is proposed here in a spirit of homage to many of the music makers and troubadours of the recent past. Their decisive output sustained an oppositional tradition through inhospitable times, and they were part of a desegregation generation that has begun to die out. The extent to which their deaths have been uneulogised and unmourned has been bewildering to me. The official archives of African American cultural and musical history extend no further than a ritual veneration of those aspects of jazz which are judged to be en route toward the Emerald City of a properly classical, "racial" culture. Eight decades ago, Locke had identified that possibility as "super-jazz."[3]

The act of salvage humbly proposed here requires not only a renewed

attention to the vernacular achievements of responsible leaders like
Curtis, but also an appreciation of their unheralded supporting musicians. For every instrumental genius like the great bass player James
Jamerson who finds a degree of belated or posthumous recognition,
there are many others whose faces and contributions remain unknown.
I emphasise this to underscore a point I have made before. A virtuous
rapport with the presence of death was one key characteristic of the tradition of music making *towards freedom* which is now coming to an end,
as the freedom to consume without limit promises the satisfaction of all
desires. There were elusive mechanisms connecting that rapport to a
critique of capitalism and its corrosive reification of a culture which was
always more important to its makers and users than merely being a matter of individual life and death. Even if that link between the various attributes of this disposition was a contingent one, it was fortuitous. It is
now something that is worth actively remembering.

The debt owed by this art to a deliberately heightened awareness of
death, loss, and suffering betrays and affirms a different axiology—an
alternative system of judgement and value—that was not only incompatible with the indices of the capitalist market, but deeply opposed to
them. Though the aspiration towards authentic freedom did coexist with
market relations, the stresses involved in their coming together were
always apparent. Here again, Curtis Mayfield's tactics repay careful
study. The angry pedagogy of his soundtrack to the blaxploitation film
Superfly provides a paradigmatic instance of how that recurrent conflict
might be contained and managed in the interest of everyday virtue and
dissenting thought. In those days, film soundtracks were usually recorded by a single artist or group. Soundtrack albums from the Seventies like "Come Back Charleston Blue," "Let's Do It Again," or "Sparkle"
constructed a relationship between sound and image that differed from
the one we know through more recent exercises in cross-platform marketing and brand synergy, in which the music is relegated to the role of
background design or mnemonic trigger. In the first instance, the mu-

sic was produced to be bought afterwards in order for the listener to recall and savour aspects of the film in a world before video recording.
It could also carry news of the film as a cultural event to groups of consumers who might otherwise have been hard to reach. Today, the sedi-
mented meaning borne by those old songs is placed in films in order
to invest them with a profundity and emotional force that they spontaneously lack. Recent creations like "Are We There Yet?" "Friday," and
"Phat Girlz" all provide good examples. This change invites us to take
account of the disaggregation and iconisation of the old rebel culture
and to identify the collusion of its contemporary administrators—or at
least those who control its copyright and image rights—with media
cheerleaders and their industry henchpeople: the ethnic brokers and
project-managing pimps of corporate multiculturalism.

I want to register a protest against the fragmentation of that expressive, freedom-seeking cultural tradition in the name of its currency in
ever-wider markets, against any fatal complicity in the denial of the
musical forms' own rich history, and against the systematic erasure of
historical patterns in the relationship between past and present. Iconisation and fragmentation have an impact on the workings of memory.
Icons, like logos, are made to be unforgettable. They are visual cues that
make the difficult work of recollection into the very different activity of
linear association.

Making the past audible in the present has been a customary musical
practice. It never proceeded in straight lines. The work of others—chosen ancestors and creative kin—was always cited. Musical events and
vocabularies of different kinds were quoted and connected in unanticipated ways. These traditional gestures could be ironic or ludic, respect-
ful or parricidal. They constituted an aesthetic style and provided an
evolving frame for a creative daring which can be evident only in the
moment. That historic system now also appears to be in retreat.

Today, we encounter music between two poles which can be represented in simplified form as a choice between clear alternatives. The

first is a simple recycling of old ideas which looks superficially like the continuation of vital tradition. In fact, it is something else because it operates without the pleasures that arose from the simultaneous discovery of the forms that are being reaffirmed by people who have not themselves made any contribution to their development. This activity can be pleasurable and fits tidily with established patterns of musical training and the idea of a standard repertoire. The second strategy employs effectively deskilled, dehumanised technologies which, along with indifference, laziness, and disregard, have reduced a shocking modernist tradition to a tame lexicon of preconstituted fragments. The first stance can be called the Marsalis or Lincoln Center option. It fetishises technique to produce a sham authenticity from the hard labour of mastering the preferred techniques and approved vocabularies. The second strategy—we can call this the DJ or hip hop option—uses the new technology to make the negative labour involved in technical mastery instantly redundant. Both of these options have their own characteristic patterns of pseudo-commemoration, and each of them promotes an uncomplicated variety of nonspecific pastness to offset the manufactured immediacy demanded by insatiable consumer culture. These conflicting tendencies may yet be reconciled in the aesthetics of the mashup; however, I am asking for a negative verdict on the culture of simulation that requires music and its pleasures to be moved from the privileged space they had acquired at the core of the cultural conversation that made black Atlantic history and sociality. Today, that music often becomes nothing more than a source of components for a dubious soundtrack contrived to support an even more questionable flow of video images.

Ethical losses resulted from marginalising the intersubjective, antiphonal equilibrium that had been practised in ritual real-time collaboration between performers and crowds. Centring musical creation on computer screens compounded these difficulties. The resulting music has sometimes celebrated the expulsion of any trace of fallible and funky humanity. The sinuous warmth of real-time bass and drums was often surplus to requirements.

We should not be surprised if the "regression of listening" is an idea that springs to mind when considering the consequences of this shift.[4] There is regression in the obvious sense that ears are no longer being conditioned to the possibility of distinguishing the sampled and simulated from the played. Sequenced and quantised sounds become indistinguishable from the older but still-supple forms of interactivity that characterised music made in a culture of listening for a community of listeners, rather than an aggregation of shoppers, downloaders, and headphoned poddies. The end of that version of interpretive community has been associated with the decline of publicity—that is, with the decay and retreat of a public sphere. Raymond Williams was, as we have seen, prescient about the consequences of "mobile privatisation," but he did not have to reckon with the fact that the wholesale privatisation of culture transformed the mechanisms of social memory. A culture of loneliness—not merely of isolation or solitude—accompanied this change and now fosters a yearning for forms of sociality to which the market aims to provide ready-made solutions. The coltan-fuelled mobile phone and the omnipresent computer screen are the favoured portals through which repair and recovery are to be transacted. The software for this exercise is largely, though not completely, the product of recent African American culture produced during the thirty-five-year life of hip hop.[5] It is therefore time to reconsider the characteristics of that culture in the period before hip hop.

Along the Watchtower

There is a sense in which Jimi Hendrix tried to win recognition as a black American and failed. Though his futuristic art would eventually be credentialed as the characteristic product of racial and national genius, it was, like Miles Davis' once-despised "electric" recordings, largely unappreciated by his countrymen and -women at the time it was produced. That time-lag in the comprehension and acceptance of his innovations is important. Many of Hendrix's immortal articulations of the slave sublime, transposed into genre-defying statements of human suffering, yearning, and hope, were, after all, created far from his birthplace, his homeland, and his kin.

His short life reveals so many inspired transgressions of redundant musical and racial rules that it is hard to know where to commence. Seattle, New York, and swinging London all provide promising points of departure. Each accents his life in significant ways, but none of them is adequate to carry its full weight or represent that itinerant existence properly in its beautiful, liquid complexity.

Counterpointing the gypsy life that Hendrix celebrated and attempted to moralise, his music demands that any convincing critical engagement with its composer become polycentric. This point was underlined by the Brazilian Caetano Veloso's provocative description of Jimi's musical creations as "half blues, half Stockhausen." He continued: "With Hendrix, all fundamental themes could be radicalized. But there was too much confusion in his sound for my taste, too many cymbals, too much 'jazz.'"[6]

If we are to make sense of that hybrid, we have to be as able as Hendrix was to accommodate the absorption of the very different disciplines that were inculcated in him by the U.S. Army, the South, and the chitlin circuit. The bad sign under which he was born should be recognised as a complex constellation. It involved a deep and abiding ambivalence about being racialised at all, never mind being 'buked, scorned, and Jim Crowed as an African American. There are ethnocentric pressures to be resisted and a whole lot of well-intentioned but unhelpful mystification that belittles Jimi by making him superhuman—somebody who did not have to work or practice in order to achieve greatness. Just the sheer patient labor involved in his revolution makes his music something more than an intuitive or wholly instinctive emanation of collective black American being in the world.

That said, we must start with the blues because that is where he started. But we should not get trapped there on the threshold of the red house they accommodate. We depart from that dwelling place to gain a better appreciation of how Jimi playfully possessed the blues and amended its workings so that they would be adequate to the technological and moral challenges arising from the unsettled cultural environment of the decolonising Cold War world. We must see how he managed to overcome tradition's constraints, twisting them into creative opportunities, electrifying them, blending and bending them into different registers of protest and affirmation. He was always prepared creatively to damage the superficial integrity of the musical idioms in which he located himself. A modernist desire to destroy and shock was pivotal, and it was not just confined to what Hendrix did in the act of performing on stage.

Gypsy that he was, Hendrix said he wanted to be buried in England, his adopted homeland. Yet one of his greatest moments as a performer was the 1969 Woodstock Festival's systematically artful assault upon the patriotic musical heart of the imperial nation in whose paratroops he had previously served with pride. It was then hell-bent upon destroying the Vietcong with the same fervour that currently guides its impossible and interminable "war on terror." Through the exemplary boldness—a quality Jimi linked to love—with which he separated himself from those armed forces, we can understand what was at stake in the unfolding of a cultural revolution that deliberately and self-consciously drew its poetry and its soundscape from the future.

Hendrix's reaching for not just the future, but a more philosophically coherent "not-yet," unsettled his contemporaries and continues to confound critics. That assertively utopian quality is what still enables his work to speak so powerfully. It was a product of his desire to avoid what the previous generation of blues people had done: mournfully to interact with the sunrise of the next day by serenading it, greeting every condemnation to prolonged suffering in the industrialised valley of the dry bones with resignation and defiance. Albert King, whose epochal

"Blues at Sunrise" could be taken as the limit of that exhilarating approach, was famed as a driver on construction sites.[7] His legend says he could pick up a carpet delicately with his bulldozer. Jimi, no habitué of the killing floor, seems only ever to have been a soldier and a musician. His deep alienation and his sense of what work could be and where it stood in relation to the freedoms that were necessary in order to feel free, stone free, were utterly different.

The primal scene of Jimi's existential encounter with the prospect of radical autonomy was still dawn, the approved neo-traditional staging. Yet unlike Albert, from whom he had drawn such compelling inspiration, Jimi aimed to articulate musical sound that could approximate the power of those first rays in reilluminating and perhaps reenchanting the world. In other words, Jimi's utopian yearning for a different, peaceful future was associated with his turn towards myth.

It is easy to miss the full significance of this by just saying that Hendrix was ahead of his time or that it has taken thirty or forty years to catch up with his cosmopolitan Afro-futurism. A lengthy period was required to make his technical departures part of the standard repertoire of his instrument. Comments on his "avant-garde" position reveal fragments of a larger truth; yet the substantive issue is not that Hendrix was ahead, but rather that he was able to pronounce another time—sculpting temporality itself so that his listeners could, in effect, be transported from one time to another. This marks a significant shift out of the temporality in which the dialectical mechanism of "double consciousness" could be used to resolve the pressures of contending loyalties, identities, and forms of affect. Here, in a pattern that differs sharply from the trajectories Du Bois and Locke had anticipated, African American music would become enigmatic with regard to its approved teleology.

This move was not the chance result of the fact that Jimi's ascent coincided with the appearance of an oppositional and curious youth culture to which recreational drugs were fundamental. The gloriously damaged sound of his first songs announced and then enacted the impact

of a colorful counter-culture that beat back the monochrome tones in
which a grey, decaying (Jimi would probably have said "plastic") world
had been enveloped. A massive gesture of refusal was distilled in the
anthemic, insubordinate chorus of "If Six Was Nine," but it was evident
everywhere: in his Kings Road dandyism, in his characteristic mixture
of politeness and assertiveness, and in his appetite for those theatrical,
"auto-destructive" performances. I remember the impact of those daring, wild, and dissonant opening notes of "Purple Haze" which hit the
airwaves in England in the spring of 1967 just as I was starting to become interested in becoming a guitar player myself. The line "Lately
things just don't seem the same," coupled with the singer's apparent
ease of access to the sky on which he would bestow his kiss, confirmed
the same epoch-making novelty. Things were suddenly and dramati-
cally different. To my awestruck ears, the question "Are You Experienced?" gave thrilling voice to a cataclysmic, intergenerational rupture.
It was only later that I could begin to interpret the change trumpeted
there as involving more than generational antagonisms. The blues was
audibly present, but this was not a Lightnin' Hopkins record or the ar-
chaic, beautiful fruit of some Lomaxian, ethnomusicological excursion
down to Stovall's Plantation. Blues moods seemed to have been transformed in an act of daring which, as Veloso's comment revealed, was
also instrumental in commanding the attention of distant, transnational audiences. These were often remote, dissenting listeners who
knew that six might indeed become nine without touching the quality of
their fragile existence on the proliferating margins of the overdeveloped world and its abbreviated freedoms, both personal and political.

   This approach to specifying the enduring significance of Hendrix's
art as a fiery, insistent pulse within a novel, dissident culture runs counter to all the sentimental approaches that strive to folksify his very
twentieth-century legacy, to imprison it in the blues that supplied both
its launch pad and its ballast, to confine it to the borders of the United
States or make it all roots and no routes, all voodoo chile and no highway

chile. Those interpretive impulses should be resisted in the names of the global network that he helped to animate and the non-national forms of blackness, and of humanity, that he shaped on his journey from soldier to troubadour.

We must therefore always think of Hendrix as an ex-paratrooper who gradually became an advocate of peace in an act of treason so profound and complete that it would make him an enemy of power until this day. I was reflecting upon the continuing moral import of that trajectory as I stood at Jimi's windswept grave on the outskirts of Seattle, accompanied only by a dignified young man in military uniform who told me that he passed his interminable days listening to Hendrix MP3s on the computer in the local army recruiting station where he worked, blankly servicing the war on terror.

Jimi's bold choice of peace and love instead of war was coupled with implacable opposition to the absurd and destructive "ego scene" that official politics had become. His understanding of that historic blend made him a marked man and a new man. It was conveyed with startling clarity as he sat wearing his light-blue silk kimono, shyly reassuring Dick Cavett that his recent transformation of "The Star Spangled Banner" had been not only beautiful but also an entirely routine happening. "We used to sing it at school," he explained in a downbeat tone.

Talking back to Frantz Fanon's theories of violence and revolution at about the same time Jimi moved to England, Martin Luther King Jr. had responded forthrightly to what he saw as the growing gains of the Black Power movement. Its adherents, he noted wistfully, were not quoting Tolstoy and Gandhi. King identified Fanon's *Wretched of the Earth* as the bible of a new political generation. In response to its appeal, King made his pacifist consideration of the issue of self-defence a practical one centred on the issue of effectiveness and the related problem of how avowedly nonviolent demonstrations should actually be conducted. Rather than seeing the struggle of African Americans as a version of national liberation, King maintained the connection of black America to the colonial world but inverted it so that African Americans could take full advantage of their uniquely endo-colonial location and start to act on behalf of others, rather than merely imitate them: "The hope of the people of color in the world may well rest on the American Negro and his ability to reform the structure of racist imperialism from within and thereby turn the technology and wealth of the west to the task of liberating the world from want."[8]

King deepened this critical engagement with Fanon's ideas. He moved the debate away from political tactics and towards a discussion of political ethics prompted by what he calls the "brave and challenging words" to be found in the concluding pages of *The Wretched of the Earth*. This change of tack revealed an interesting area of overlap in their respective analyses. "The problem is that Fanon . . . [is proceeding] with a willingness to imitate old concepts of violence. . . . This is one thing about modern civilisation that I do not care to imitate." King argued instead that the choice of love required a special strength and that the effort was worthwhile because it would pay a special dividend. He continued: "Humanity is waiting for something other than blind imitation of the past. If we want to advance a step further, if we want to turn over a new leaf and really set a new man afoot, we must begin to turn mankind away from the long and desolate night of violence. May it not be that the new man the world needs is the nonviolent man? . . . A dark, desperate, confused and sin-sick world waits for this new kind of man and this new kind of power."[9]

Here is the sound of the future being enlisted in the struggle against racism, which was identified with precision as a conflict over the nature of masculinity. At that moment, tomorrow seemed to be on the side of those who wanted to enhance democracy. Inequality, callousness, and merciless economic exploitation were briefly but powerfully being associated with the past. Their presence was experienced fleetingly as outmoded. The instrumental "Third Stone from the Sun" is an abiding example of how Jimi made the same revolutionary feeling audible and attractive.

The night that news of King's murder reached the Jimi Hendrix Experience, they were due to play a concert in Newark. The streets were silent and deserted, and the local police anxious in case cancellation of the show would contribute to a volatile atmosphere. The band was supported by the British group Soft Machine, whose lighting technician, the Scottish artist and painter Mark Boyle, described the event:

> Hendrix came out to immense applause and said, "This number is for a friend of mine." . . . He abandoned completely his normal set. The band played an improvisation which was absolutely, hauntingly beautiful. Immediately everybody knew what this was about. This was a lament for Martin Luther King. Within minutes the whole audience was weeping. . . . Old redneck stagehands came to the side of stage and they were standing there with tears streaming down their faces. The music had a kind of appalling beauty. Harrowing music. When he came to the end, there was no applause.[10]

That wordless exercise in mourning contrasts sharply with the situation that developed a couple of years later. By then, an even bolder Jimi had started to find a more complex and consistently satisfying equilibrium between his poetry and his music. The song "House Burning Down" was still a long way from "Freedom," his mature, posthumously released restatement of the problem; but encoded as it was, it articulated an urgent warning. It provides an intriguing instance of how his most portentous and mythical lyrics could ask tough, demanding questions about the ethics of care in a segregated society, while his music referred listeners not only to the alternative possibilities of the not-yet, but to what he imagined were higher and better ways of existing in harmony with themselves, their environments, and each other. That song articulated Hendrix's response to the historical injunction "Burn Baby Burn." It involved more than an obvious warning against self-destruction. He suggests an analysis of what had triggered rage and violence, but much more significant was his coded account of how the effects of black America's riotous protest reached him in distant, tea-sipping England and compelled him to return and investigate the events. Distance and estrangement are conveyed in his account of an uncomfortable encounter with the fratricidal mob. The mythic staging of what sounds like a cry of perplexed and defeated rage against the violence of a pogrom also elevated a deliberately obscure reading of America's domestic conflicts to cosmic significance.[11] A space boat eventually lands with "eerie grace" to take away the bodies of the dead, and thus the message to love became a message to the universe. A planetary vision supplied Jimi's global mindset with a suitably futuristic vehicle for its existential critique of a world soured and defiled by racial hierarchy. This scenario was not a routine result of some New Age occult impulse. These were properly historical moods, tied to a new iconic immediacy of the planet, that had been captured for the first time from outside Earth's orbit by cameras on the Apollo spacecraft in 1968. Strictly speaking, this was a planetary rather than a cosmic consciousness, and it seems also to have been derived straightforwardly from Jimi's repudiation of the belligerent geopolitical mission that young men like himself were then routinely being given in Southeast Asia by Uncle Sam.

It's worth repeating that Hendrix, who may have been a far better soldier than the official PR machine suggests, joined and then left the army. He acquired a subtle antipathy towards the military mentality, which was rewired and then reworked as the target of all his hopes for a better world. His personal journey towards peace was all the more convincing because it is clear that his conversion to that cause had been gradual, and because along the way he had discovered the pleasures of jumping out of airborne war machines and falling through the sky. Perhaps that ontological shaking and sustained closeness of death also nudged him towards mythic responses. They certainly seem to have fostered an update in the poetics of world citizenship and induced him to imagine taming the military-industrial complex through the subversive act of travel by dragonfly rather than plane or helicopter.

The self-conscious myth-making was part of the otherworldliness.

Its results are broader and brighter-hued than the safer, unconvincing cosmography of the worn-out Christianity they aimed first to undo and then to supplant.

Hendrix's exit velocity from the Vietnam-era U.S. military enabled him to borrow the arrows of desire from William Blake's Muggletonian quiver and bravely put them to work opposing both neo-imperial war and moribund politics. The unpatriotic decision to choose peace and espouse nonviolence was offset by the tense and difficult relationship Hendrix enjoyed with his manager, Michael Jeffrey, the mysterious and ruthless Newcastle-based gangster who sometimes boasted of his own military activities in the murkiest depths of the colonial warfare to which Britain's secret state had committed the ailing, no-longer-imperial country. It is said that Jeffrey carried a Beretta pistol in a "stylish kidskin shoulder holster," could speak Russian, and had been stationed in Egypt during the Suez crisis of 1956.[12] He does seem to have worked for British Intelligence in some capacity.[13]

While bravely opposing the war in Indochina, Hendrix managed to confound and disappoint anybody who wanted him to adopt conventional or facile political views and to enrage anyone who found his elliptical pronouncements on ethics, history, and governmentality too much to stomach. What we identify as environmentalist or green themes in his work should be acknowledged as an additional measure of the global scale of his anxieties about the fate of humankind. The prospect of larger tragedies involved in species death looms over his explorations of the contingency, tragedy, and brevity of fragile human life. His repeated references to native Americans are part of this alternative cosmology, but it remains a mood rather than a program—and perhaps it is all the more powerful for that. There is only a Cherokee mist, the lingering trace of an indigenous, non-European sensibility, veiled in musical fog, swirling wordlessly with a spiritual energy drawn from the dopplered, harmonically unstable notes that are flying out from the spinning speakers of his Leslie cabinet. That trail of tears, the suffering in that genocide, and the misery of reservation containment must all stay wordless if they are to retain their power to inspire, humble, and shame. In the bared teeth of this unspeakable history, words come too cheaply. Jimi's transethnic turn is neither a willful drift away from blackness into exoticism nor a belated, programmatic bid to set history straight by invoking an interplanetary Seminole genealogy. The tragic outcome—the castle made of sand—refers us to the enduring presence of alternative possibilities. Another world is possible. Jimi conjures up the prospect of it (in Ernst Bloch's terms)—a castle in the air—and says that the resources for building that utopia are, unexpectedly and magically, already at hand.[14] Early in his career, they could be glimpsed nightly at Seattle's Spanish Castle.

To forget America's internal tragedies and the genocide of its conquest and expansion would be to deny the uniqueness of its hybrid identity, and in so doing to sustain the passivity and renunciation which corrupt and inauthentic power relies upon. Opposing the alienated submissiveness that has been engineered from above required recognising the catastrophe of America's colonial progress. In turn, that acceptance became part of acquiring the machinery of liberation. The pursuit of an alternative future necessitates the cultivation of counter-memory. Even time, as Herbert Marcuse put it, "loses its power when remembrance redeems the past."[15]

The significance of Hendrix's many creative transgressions has been multiplied not only by the brevity of his life, but also by a sense of its radical incompleteness. This has encouraged critics to project images of him that are burdened and trapped by their own preoccupations. Rather than place Hendrix inside somebody else's dubious fantasy of what his music ought to have been, it seems to make more sense to treat his own artistic aspirations for his work more seriously, to reconstruct them in their historical settings and see whether, like his calculated refusal of shallow and trivial political language, they might help to explain why his music would not die along with him. Accordingly, I have tried to take

both Jimi's appetite for utopian and mythic themes and his tacit, antipolitical politics more seriously than is currently conventional.

Just as with Marley, Jimi's strange immortality has made his media
afterimage unusually plastic and mutable. It may be better to accept that
final evaluations of his boldness are impossible and to argue that understanding his music and its enduring popularity involves a number of
historical and cultural puzzles. Once again as in Marley's case, the art's
life after Jimi's death is rather more than a narrowly aesthetic matter. It
raises a number of delicate interpretive problems that have the power
to detonate all overly simple models of African American culture and
identity and redirect us to a number of neglected issues. Among the
more important are the history and phenomenology of the electric guitar, a consideration of the pivotal point where music making became a
matter of electronic sound, and the interesting tale of how innovations
derived from military research found peaceful uses in the emergent
realm of musical sound-processing technology. The use of the Univibe—
an early pedal-based phase shifter that simulated Doppler effects—on
the historic Band of Gypsys recording "Machine Gun" provides the best
example of that particular irony.

Unexpected links between peace and war oblige us to answer a host of
difficult inquiries about the Cold War's cultural dimensions, about the
combined and uneven development of global markets for racialised,
popular cultural products, and about the commercial value of video immortality. Before we can even pose questions of that order, we are also
required to ask: What version of black cultural history might Hendrix's
gypsy life be used to construct? The repeated affirmation of itinerancy
cannot be erased. Jimi's poetry of transience presents life as a journey
without an arrival. His romanticism is betrayed by the projection of a
self that is "essentially a traveller—a questing, homeless self whose
standards derive from, [and] whose citizenship is of, a place that does
not exist at all or yet, or no longer exists; one consciously understood as
an ideal, opposed to something real. . . . The journey is unending and

the destination, therefore, negotiable."[16] We need to understand where
existing frameworks which defer too readily to the boundaries of national states, or are inclined to respect the disciplinary authority of
those who claim to know the proper course of national cultures, might
have to be amended in order to make sense of the fluctuations and de-
tours that have surrounded and nurtured this itinerant art. We need to
grasp how Hendrix's music has not only retained its special power but
grown in stature, acquiring a new significance that lets it speak to several different generations of listeners, especially the more recent and
remote audiences for whom the blues is not a primary point of musical
reference. They have found their way back to Hendrix nonetheless, both
because of the way that his musical imagination saturated the scene even
as the electric guitar moved out of the central position he won for it, and
because of the way that his life and art pose an elemental choice between
war and peace which remains sadly relevant.

The blues is not usually thought of as a modernist form. Its electrification has not been very well understood, appearing more usually as a
linear development of unyielding traditions that are predictable and
knowable. The standard script runs like this. Blasted out from the plantations where it had been formed, the blues was dispatched northwards
into the accelerated, vertiginous, and abject modernity of America's
segregated cities. That degraded and degrading metropolitan environment had been memorably explored by Richard Wright, along with a selection of Edwin Rosskam's photographs, in their historic collaboration
Twelve Million Black Voices, published in 1941, just a year before Jimi was
born. Wright, an autodidact, philosopher-sociologist, and renegade
postal worker as well as a writer, was the first African American chroni-
cler of this novel urban tragedy to reach for the concept of modernity in
order to make sense of what he was seeing in the iconic kitchenettes and
alleys of Chicago's South Side. That racialised geography, where Jimi
was never more than a brief visitor, provided a heated environment in
which modernist adaptations of the form would be forged. There, the

custodianship of black culture was reinvested in the newly arrived urban populations that never quite managed to stand in for their rural antecedents.

While other aspects of black vernacular existence were in terrible flux, the blues was somehow able to resist the turbulence. Critical orthodoxy says that from that historic point, the form itself did not really change. Perhaps its development had been arrested by the extreme shock of racially stratified hypermodernity. Just a few years after Hendrix died (scratching at a phased Stratocaster to complete the detour that "Red House" had begun), the cryptically postmodern playing of Albert King announced the absolute invariance of the music while slyly celebrating the very mutability that his words denied.[17] Answering the conservative inclinations of the voices that prize sedentary culture above the itinerant and feral forms with which it is often in conflict, this counter-history of black identities and identifications says that Jimi came along and changed the game. His intervention showed where tradition was not a simple repetition but a reflexive practice of custom that leaned towards the liberationist possibilities of the not-yet by valorising a combination of "flexibility in substance and formal adherence to precedent."[18]

Wright's account of Chicago life associated modernity with cultural and existential complexity, and saw how the experiential discrepancy visible along America's racial fault line had to be made intelligible. This was to be accomplished not in the synchronised pattern of Du Bois's double consciousness, which had been absorbed too easily, but non-synchronously as a temporal disjunction. Wright described the process thus, in a passage which still generates fierce critical debate: "More than even that of the American Indian, the consciousness of vast sections of our black women lies beyond the boundaries of the modern world, though they live and work in that world daily."[19] Wright's acute and thoughtful analysis of this temporal and historical fracture offered two other telling comments on the black world that was coming into being inside the ghetto walls. He confides, "There are times when we doubt our songs"; and then, with the help of one of Rosskam's most poignant pictures to underscore the haunting point, he adds wearily, "Strange moods fill our children." That was the broken world in which Jimi was raised and to which his revolutionary art responded with the subversive aim of reenchantment.

From this oblique angle, Jimi might now reappear attractively as a prodigal heir to the comparable revolutionary legacies of Robert Johnson and Charlie Christian, two other African American guitar geniuses that the wider world still pays attention to. Their combination of musical innovations triangulates our reconstituted, transblack tradition. Johnson provides one axis of Hendrix's world by marking the historic transition of everyday blues art into the altered tempos of the industrial age. That fatal crossroads is only one of a number of special sites where tradition and modernity intersected, or, more accurately, where two discrepant modernities—one of the plantation and the other of the metropolis—came into exhilarating and troubling contact.

Johnson's favoured deity was the devil, but not the vengeful Old Testament presence of Afro-Baptist lore. The spirits which haunted his melancholy art inhabited a profane world in which the order of racial terror remained dominant even after slavery was abolished. Yet that system had started to shift and crack in response to demands for new varieties of freedom. Accordingly, God retreated to a new position and theodicy assumed a different character. Negroes who had previously walked with Jesus had started to learn to drive. There was no crosstown traffic in Clarkesdale Mississippi, so Johnson likened the body of his lover to a Terraplane car. His audience understood what he meant when he announced that he wanted to check the oil and get under the hood. The railroad had yielded up its special poetic place to the speed and style of the private automobile. Henry Ford's automotive commodities became infused with libidinal energy, and downpressed people could embrace their alienation as the starting point for existential challenges premised upon their understanding of themselves and their fates as "a mirror of all the manifold experiences of America."[20]

The elemental force of Johnson's life is a complicated thing, even if we must reject the occult suggestion that Hendrix was conceived close to the moment of the older man's murder. We need to make some space for the mediating figure of Muddy Waters and acknowledge his mainstreaming of the blues; but the other axis of Jimi's world is most usefully identified with the youthful figure of Christian, who did far more than merely reveal where the distinctive musical language of the electrified guitar might commence. Making a moving and insightful consideration of his classmate's revolutionary musical achievements in giving the amplified instrument its jazz voice, Ralph Ellison described the emergence, within and around the music, of a ritual space where a real, rehumanising pleasure could be derived from elemental contests in which "each artist challenges all the rest; [and] each solo flight or improvisation represents (like the canvases of a painter) a definition of his identity: as individual, as member of the collectivity and as a link in the chain of tradition."[21] Setting aside Jimi's doubts about whether his own music could or should be described as jazz, we can consider whether he fits into that famous definition of the jazz-making process.

Like both of the imaginary guitarist-ancestors I have given him, Jimi certainly subscribed to endless improvisation on and reconstruction of traditional materials. But like Ellison's proto-bebopping Christian, the man who liberated the guitar from the rhythm section, Hendrix was absolutely prepared to lose his identity even in the process of finding it. He can therefore be thought of as both victim and beneficiary of the conflict between his instrument's existing technical vocabulary and its adequacy as a means to represent "those sounds which form a musical definition of Negro American experience."[22]

Du Bois had used what he called "sorrow songs" to frame his idea of double consciousness: two warring souls, one Negro and one American, locked adversarily in a single dark body on the way towards synthesis as "a higher, better self." His linkage suggests that these "ethnic" sounds were already becoming harder to identify, distinguish, and isolate from the other contending soundscapes of the modern United States, even at the dawn of the twentieth century. Since then, the desire to make music into the medium of cultural rebirth and to hear in it the characteristic signature of racial genius was a recurrent feature of critical thinking about black culture. Naming and positioning black music in this way was, it seems, a significant element in bringing about that very result.

For a while, music did occupy the epicentre of black culture in a new and distinctively modern way: as both custom and commodity. Although black art gradually and painfully separated itself from the tempo of black life, music remained a potent means to connect understanding of the new era to important, identity-building reflections on the simpler un-freedoms that had preceded it. These historical observations generate an objection to Ralph Ellison's implicit complacency and rather narrow specifications of what could officially count as jazz. Yet once we appreci-ate the double character of African American music, we are delivered into a new interpretive territory equally distant from assimilationist schemes and all putatively Afrocentric musings about the relationship between trumpet mutes, sink plungers, and wah-wah pedals.

Jimi's musical visions demanded sonic and technological changes. They seized on the Leslie speaker and other related innovations like the Univibe, which employed light to destabilise and alter the phasing of sounds. These and many other features of Jimi's sonic revolution de-serve more attention than they get when they are misconceived as sim-ple, preprogrammed effects of the attenuated African survivals with which they are in such complex dialogue.

With one ear turned back towards Du Bois, Alain Locke had identified these problems as early as 1936, many years before Jimi climbed aboard his eagle's wing. This is what Locke wrote: "Jazz in its most serious form, has also become the characteristic musical speech of the modern age. . . . It incorporated the typical American restlessness and unconventionality, embodied its revolt against the drabness of commonplace life, put pagan force behind the revolt against Puritan restraint, and finally became the western world's life-saving flight from boredom and over-sophistication to the refuge of elemental emotion and primitive vigor."[23] Locke's insight identified music with doubling of a different variety: that of the dialectical scheme Du Bois had borrowed from Germany.

The evolution of culture had ceased to be comprehensible as a simple matter of approved consciousness being distributed evenly into the willing receptacles that even divided racial souls provide. This discomforting development presented the exponential doubling of untidily folded selves in a fissured, pleated culture. Now it affords us with a means to reframe the internality of racial identity without presupposing either essence or interiority: "Folds incorporate without totalizing, internalize without unifying, collect together discontinuously in the form of pleats making surfaces, spaces, flows and relations."[24] Doesn't the multitracked guitar onslaught on our senses that Jimi orchestrated for the opening sections of "Ezy Rider" take us past the place where the idea of the original ceases to be worthwhile? In the multiplicity of swirls and screams, the issue of which track was laid down first starts to be irrelevant. The overall effect of their orchestrated combination becomes more important. Jimi's guitar howls and is multiplied, chorused into a dynamic sonic image of unprecedented plurality. Its constantly shifting screams betoken a new conception of irreducibly complex identity.

Ellison's argument about Charlie Christian is relevant here also because it carefully positioned the guitarist's inventiveness on his recently amplified instrument between the poles of entertainment and experience. We can map those options onto the split between Hendrix the minstrel showman and Hendrix the immobile, serious musician, the shamanic pastor of the partly hidden public world he called the "electric church."

In explaining artistic choices that felt eccentric then but seem so no longer, Hendrix spoke about that ecumenical congregation from time to time. It was a collective social body of musical celebrants that gathered periodically to engage the amplified offshoots of the Mississippi Delta and harness them in the causes of human creativity and liberation. Its ritual events had become loud, he told Cavett in the same July 1969 interview, not only because the appalling state of the world meant that many people needed to be jolted awake by the shock that only elevated volume could supply, but also because, if the wakeup call could be delivered on the correct frequency, it might in turn promote a direct encounter with the souls of the listeners. Here, Du Bois's sense of where sorrowful, transcendent music augmented the power of words and writing supplies an active presence, though Hendrix's comment suggests a departure from the savant's more conventional, and by then rather outdated, understanding of the workings of the embattled black public sphere. Hendrix's career tells us that by this point, black music could produce its own public world: a social corona that could nourish or host an alternative sensibility, a structure of feeling that might function to make wrongs and injustices more bearable in the short term but could also promote a sense of different possibilities, providing healing glimpses of an alternative moral, artistic, and political order.

The electric church was of a piece with the wider revolutionary upsurge of that moment. The traditional celebrations of Afro-baptism, secularised, profaned, and fragmented, had been adapted to the larger task of community defence. Under the banners of Black Power and anticolonial solidarity, its irregular services began to alter the political mentality of black peoples worldwide and to transform and even synchronise understanding of their emergent place in postcolonial conditions. This could be done without a recognisably political word being spoken aloud. The church's fundamentally oppositional character was disguised by its intimate relationship with the music and dance with which happy Negroes had appeared to reaffirm their infra-human nature.

The dualistic pairing of the showman and the serious musician can be used to reveal yet another take on the shifting dimensions of residual double consciousness. But I hope to have suggested that dualism is neither appropriate nor sufficient. Jimi reinforces that verdict by moving our sensoria away from the basic stereophony of his first recordings towards the raging would-be three-dimensionality of the later work.

A larger mapping of where Hendrix might be made over in order to fit the topography of an expanded jazz tradition and a reconceptualised grasp of the electric guitar is urgently needed.[25] We can locate him in relation to the neglected contributions of Grant Green, Sonny Sharrock, and Kenny Burrell, as well as those of Albert King, Steve Cropper, and Curtis Mayfield. We can draw upon the wisdom of B. B. King to show where Jimi found the ball,[26] and seek out the contemporary commentaries of figures like Guthrie Govan and Allan Holdsworth to identify where he left it. But as people turn away from the electric guitar and towards the DJ's decks and the creative possibilities of software like Ableton Live, that sort of archaeological operation has its limits.

Hendrix was somebody who occasionally checked into his many hotel rooms under the name H. Bean. This should not be overlooked, or inflated into a self-conscious bid for overdue recognition as human. It is just another small clue that can help us to comprehend what is at stake in the basic metaphysical question that reverberates unashamedly throughout his work. That question is, "What does it take to be heard?"

In judging Hendrix today as an immortal icon in a video-saturated occularcentric culture, we must remember that being heard is thankfully not the same thing as being seen. Though they can be connected, Jimi's orphic demand is not Fanon's humanist appeal for recognition—which, you may recall, had been shaped by the impact of seeing himself being seen by people whose attachment to race hierarchy meant that they could neither concede black humanity nor realise their own. The shocking power of amplified sound solicits identification differently. It dispatched or drew listeners into new bodily predicaments. They discovered themselves prosthetically. Whether that mode of being in the world was ultimately compatible with the order of race remains to be discovered. We have Jimi Hendrix's art to assist us with those urgent enquiries, and his compelling creative answer to that question was no.

The Soundtrack to Globalisation

Hendrix's example shows how studying the travels of American popular music during the twentieth century can yield a distinctive understanding of the great transformations we have become obliged to call globalisation. Transnational history complicates the economic logic which has been employed to define those complex processes. It can also disrupt the over-simple periodisation that has been provided for them so far, and it can suggest useful, if unorthodox, ideas as to what the political forms of negative globalisation may be and become in the future.

Building upon the opportunities that have fallen to me as a remote listener and user of U.S. soundscapes, I have queried the way that the history of African American music has been conceptualised—that is, primarily as a racial and national story delivered at a single, even tempo. Undoing the nationalist assumptions underpinning the writing of history highlights significant difficulties in the way that the idea of culture circulates in criticism of this music. For many commentators, there is a degree of discomfort involved in accepting how African American music and culture come to stand for the culture of the United States as a whole, and how they became enmeshed in a broader, global conflict in which they served the political and diplomatic interests of the country. There is anxiety as well as pride in the way that they have supplied the mainspring of a global youth culture, provided a cipher for U.S. freedoms, and at times furnished a compelling instantiation of its democratic hopes.

We must return to the old assumption that the musics involved in a widely defined black Atlantic history, and the disenchanted political culture that accompanies it, can be appreciated in a variety of ways. They should be prized not just for their creativity, emotional force, and artistic and technical innovations, but also politically and philosophically. Bob Marley's repeated suggestion that his music had a philosophical import provides a significant warrant for that approach. Above all, these musical traditions can be appreciated for the consistent force with which they have articulated and indeed summoned up the possibility of better worlds and pitched it against the miseries, raciological terrors, and routine wrongs of resurgent capitalist exploitation. This was done over a long period of time in a distinctive manner which bore the unlikely imprint of slavery and the burden of its negation—but that is not the main point here. The transcoding and transcendence of suffering made productive, made useful but not redemptive, should direct our attention toward the utopian possibilities those musical formations have helped to construct, enact, and make attractive, particularly with regard to the notion of human rights.

I have also argued that against the expectations of an expanding market, this dissident culture was not always amenable to being sold in the forms demanded by consumer culture and the institution of property: private or ethnic, intellectual or cultural. Music did become property under particular economic and cultural conditions, but that outcome always followed a struggle over the moral economy in which these cultural commodities circulated only ambivalently and reluctantly. At times, they resisted the reification that wanted to transform them into closed, complete objects. Now we comprehend them most deeply when we grasp the difficult, superficially chaotic pattern in which they, like both Marley and Hendrix, have transgressed against the twin obligations of rootedness and representativeness. Yet this culture was routinely reduced to property, both by those who profited from it directly and by many more who wrote about it in the hope of turning a secondary profit as it became mainstream Americana.

Methodological nationalism automatically assumes a distinctive angle of vision. In the history of the black Atlantic, that perspective has been associated with the way absolutist positions require and promote a view of culture as an essentially static process. Though they are staged in distinctive, local scenes, the necessarily profane and picaresque cultural formations of the black vernacular no longer belong exclusively to any discrete group and cannot therefore be held under ethno-historical copyright. That situation produces new interpretive problems. They promise a better account of the music and its evolution. We may even be able to understand at last how Bill Withers' "Ain't No Sunshine" mutated into Dr. Alimantado's "Best Dressed Chicken in Town," and what that inspired act of tropical translation might exemplify.

This change of direction produces a head-on collision with simple-minded ideas of ownership, appropriation, legitimacy, and authenticity, however well-intentioned they may be. Purity becomes impossible, and hybridity ceases to be the exclusive preoccupation of some imaginary postcolonial elite. Instead, it becomes a routine principle of unruly multiculture. Those paired, conflicting concepts—hybridity and purity—acquire great power when the relationship between cultural development and national interests is conceived in disciplinarian terms. They are invoked both positively and negatively when culture must be seen as uncontaminated in order to serve the political, psychological, and emotional interests of nation building. The history of black Atlantic music has suffered from that pressure, not only because advocates of anxiety-banishing, restorative, or compensatory purification routinely suppose that culture can be held as property, but also because their authoritarian projection of its irreducibly unanimist character locks them in to a host of unsatisfactory, Manichaean imperatives. They coerce us into a choice between heroic purity and decadent hybridity, between the frozen triumph of absolute, invariant difference and the defeat represented by an equally absolute and irredeemably corrupting intermixture that can only be felt as a loss. Against those options, I want to say that the history

of music teaches different lessons. It says, even now, that a world free
from racial hierarchy is there to be summoned and, perhaps, to be won.

The Limits of Double Consciousness

Much of what Du Bois foresaw at the dawn of the twentieth century has
proved to be accurate. Black Americans did indeed furnish an eager
planet with potent new conceptions of freedom. Those precious gifts
have now been widely exported. They altered the world's moral architecture. The ongoing battle against racism demands that we draw attention to that process, and in many circumstances celebrate it. I have suggested that it should become part of the official genealogy of human
rights. Yet we should not assume that the same world-historic culture of
freedom and freedom seeking can endure indefinitely. A strict assessment of its longevity and sustainability is implicit in these arguments.

I have been wondering whether that understanding of freedom is now
a residual presence. As it loses its old power, we may have to consign the
related idea of double consciousness to the nineteenth century. In other
words, double consciousness should be excluded from the ways that we
approach the pressing issues that are redefining the field of contemporary racial politics: security, citizenship, migration, multiculture, war,
identity, and human rights.

In these new circumstances, it doesn't seem productive to try to
transplant or reinvigorate the old ideas so that, for example, being a
black European or, in Britain, a "BME" (black and minority ethnic)
could be considered analogous to what being an American and a "Negro" meant when Du Bois was writing *The Souls of Black Folk* and specu-
lating about the constitutive power of the "color line." Plural consciousness and folded consciousness are suggestive notions, but today culture
is diffused through viral and virtual technologies. His simpler pattern
of basic doubling and dialectical tripling seems less sufficient than it
did even when Ellison declared that the dynamics of identification were

more complex than Du Bois had appeared to understand.[27] Appreciating this also involves an inducement to proceed with unpacking the concept of identity. In liberating it from superannuated dialectical rules, we should also strive to rehabilitate the idea of multiple identities, which has lately been made to sound so empty and banal. That formulation of selfhood needs to be reendowed with a capacity to shock.

These conceptual problems can also be posed historically. We might ask what Du Bois's life and legacy have to say to the iconic figures of U.S. president Barack Obama and former secretary of state Condoleezza Rice. Whatever their great qualities, Rice and Obama don't seem to have been either gifted with second sight or disabled by any inner doubleness. Their respective diagnoses of the contemporary United States diverge from the one proposed by Du Bois. Obama noted "the fissures of race that have characterised the American experience," but immediately qualified that observation by drawing attention to "the fluid state of identity—the leaps through time, the collision of cultures—that mark our modern life."[28] He acknowledged that racial inequalities exist, but he sees them as secondary to other dimensions of conflict that operate on scales above those of national states. Rice used the immediate aftermath of Hurricane Katrina to deliver her analysis of the continuing place of racial inequality in U.S. society. That, too, had a comparative aspect, but the basis on which her comparisons were made was the conventional teleological measure in which the United States was the future and everybody else was mired in the past:

> [The United States] is about 100 percent ahead of anyplace else in the world in issues of race. . . . And I say that absolutely, fundamentally. . . . You go to any other meeting around the world and show me the kind of diversity that you see in America's Cabinet, in America's foreign service, in America's business community, in America's journalistic community. . . . Show me that kind of diversity anyplace else in the world, and

> I'm prepared to be lectured about race. . . . We will be making a
> mistake if we let people jump to the conclusion that the United
> States has therefore not dealt with issues of race, particularly if
> you look at how issues of race are dealt with in most of the
> world.[29]

The defensive flourish in that final sentence qualified Rice's sense of
U.S. uniqueness by making the country's supposed triumph over racism
into a relative rather than absolute victory. Her combative words suggested that she understood her nation's vulnerability before global public opinion, which could not always fathom its peculiar postcolonial and
postslavery difficulties in this area. Much of the world approached the
prospect of an Obama presidency with relish precisely because it might
mean that the United States had moved into a new phase in which the
election of a "nonwhite" president could show how the historical pathology of white supremacism has been superseded.

Faced with the history of thwarted affiliation and disfigured belonging, many in the United States now regard the "war on terror" just as Du
Bois viewed World War I. It was an opportunity for African Americans to
"close ranks" and finally to acquire or operationalise their long-delayed
membership in the national community, as well as to experience the full
benefits of formal citizenship compromised for so long by the institutionalised effects of racial hierarchy.

Du Bois lived a long and complex life. He changed his ideological
commitments and political tactics repeatedly. At the end of his days, his
commitments to peace and internationalism led him into conflict with
the U.S. government over the Korean War, the Marshall Plan, NATO,
and a number of other domestic issues. Perhaps we might now read
those parts of his life as a final comment upon or even repudiation of the
double-consciousness idea. We should recall that he spent much of his
last decade without a passport, that he eventually joined the Communist
party at the age of ninety-three, that he renounced his U.S. citizenship

and embarked on a life in African exile as a citizen of Ghana. In those treacherous choices, he found a means to activate his long-held attachments to world citizenship and to world history. We are now obliged to ask what the contemporary analogs of those uncomfortable gestures might be.

Fanon Again?

That line of inquiry is crucial to making black politics more than either a U.S. family quarrel or a U.S. family romance. It returns us to debates that arose from the political pursuit of postcolonial independence and related problems generated by the desire for national liberation. It provides a stimulus to revisit Fanon's observations on race, culture, and identity. His unsettling words do not sound anachronistic in our post–Cold War time. His insights reveal him, perhaps unexpectedly, to be our contemporary. Whatever resonance his writing may have had in the past, it speaks powerfully to the political circumstances of this era: to questions of culture and multiculture, to the sociogenesis of racialised phantoms, to the cultural integrity and religious cohesion of contending civilisations, and above all to the vexed question of the human in the bitterly contested discourse of human rights. He can be read as offering a series of difficult and provocative comments on the significance of racism in social life and on the character of postcolonial politics, not only in Africa but also in all the other places where Europe's colonial crimes are vividly remembered, even if Europe itself has contrived to forget them.

Fanon's contempt for tepid responses to the employment of torture in Algeria remains potent, and his grasp of the fundamental significance of torture in the conduct of colonial warfare justifies the close study of his arguments. Some of his essays seem to have been addressed to the conjuncture after the Paris riots of 2005 and 2007, and France once again displayed its inability either to face the residual effects of its own ugly colonial past or to address the racism that distorts its political culture and so manifestly undermines its republican and democratic ideals. Apart from those provincial matters, Fanon also helps to explain how the ancient conflict between the cross and the crescent has been revived, and why it has been able to generate such powerful worldly forces. He provides a variety of conceptual tools that can be used to illuminate the larger crisis of multiculturalism—loudly declared dead after the endlessly fascinating treachery of Europe's "homegrown" terrorists was discovered and used to create the new arrangement I have termed "securitocracy."

In many parts of postcolonial Europe, the transition involved in being an immigrant has lapsed into a permanent condition that stretches across several generations of the "nonautochthonous." Fanon's guide to the blockages created by racism in European societies remains acute. His open disenchantment at the process of racialised exclusion from any meaningful mode of belonging also offers a useful introduction to the more general difficulties involved in inhabiting the impossible condition of being an "Afropean." That goal is unthinkable in a split world where Europe is aggressively coded white, and being a black intellectual is inconceivable because blackness is never allowed to be anything other than physical.

Against race and in pursuit of a humanism different from the liberal varieties common during the Cold War, Fanon insisted that blackness and whiteness had to be understood and analysed both historically and socially. The discourse that fixed those interrelated terms in political ontology, making them into what can be called terminal identities, was more than a filter through which we consider the problems of global convergence and immanence as a process of Americanisation—signalled in the athletic celebrity of superhuman twentieth-century figures like Jessie Owens, Coca Cola's first black spokesmodel, and Carl Lewis, an eager and eloquent representative of McDonalds at the 2008 Olympic games in Beijing.

Fortified Europe's contemporary multiculture marks a novel phase in the development of the black Atlantic. Oceanic slavers have given way to smaller, less seaworthy boats undertaking shorter, desperate journeys out of Africa. Fanon managed to speak to the continent's changing predicament in ways that illuminate why people wish to flee from there now. In particular, he addresses the complex dimensions of postcolonial struggles which could not have been anticipated because the pace of political change turned out to be much more rapid than expected. He was, for example, one of the first to understand the strategic place of Africa in determining the moral destiny of Atlantic modernity and its significance for undoing the colonial power which had fettered human progress and compromised Europe's brightest promises. Last, his writings offer enduring insights into the workings of racialised identity as sameness and solidarity as well as subjectivity. He directs us to the costs, for both victims and perpetrators, of operating in an "epidermalised" social and political environment where any common humanity is "amputated" and authentic interaction between people becomes almost impossible.

This bitter result, like the history of all practical raciology, involves notions of alienation and reification that are deeper than the ones Marxian tradition wrote about. In Fanon, their appearance is associated with the power of racism and colonial rule configured in a suspended dialectic of progress and catastrophe. There can be no resolution. The conspicuous power of that petrified formation is answered instead by his audacious commitment to an alternative conception of humanity reconstituted outside "race." This is something that does not endear Fanon's work to today's scholastic practitioners of the facile antihumanism and ethnic absolutism so characteristic of life on U.S. college campuses, where class-based homogeneity combines smoothly with deference to racial and ethnic particularity and with resignation to the world as it appears. Fanon disappoints that scholastic constituency by refusing to see culture as an insurmountable obstacle between groups, even if they have been racialised. He does not accept the "strategic" award of an essential innocence to the oppressed and the wretched of the earth. Their past and present sufferings confer no special nobility upon them and are not invested with redemptive insights. Suffering is just suffering, and Fanon has no patience with those who would invoke the armour of incorrigibility around national liberation struggles or minority cultures. From the start, he emphasises that racism brings out the very worst in everybody whose lives are distorted by its mirage. All the shadowy actors in the "epidermalised" world stand to lose something precious because racism and colonial rule delimit their humanity, deplete the character of their political life, and in the process sacrifice the psychological well-being of both perpetrator and victim. The effects upon them are not, of course, exactly the same, but the damage done to them is manifested in complementary forms and always involves significant losses. From the perspective of his avowedly new, nonracial and antiracist humanism, it is much easier to slip between those fatal categories. Perpetrator and victim are no longer stable or fixed roles. You may become a perpetrator precisely because you have previously been a victim—an insight that speaks powerfully to the history of reparative colonialism and to the difficult process that produces today's burgeoning legion of homegrown terrorists.

Anybody habituated to colonial society's Manichaean logic, or to the simplistic pseudo-politics that merely inverts it, will find these propositions difficult to concede. Fanon anticipates their bewildered reactions to the demand that we are obliged now not only to imagine the end of racial hierarchy but to act in accordance with a new universalism born in the idea of a reciprocal relation between different cultures and shaped by a radical, nonimmanent critique of racial orders. That hopeful, utopian formation can arise only after the end of colonial rule. Yet I believe certain emergent elements of it have been prefigured in the convivial interaction we can discover in postcolonial cities, particularly where incomers' demands for a deeper democracy have constituted a civic asset.

The critique of racial ontology that was spelled out poetically and aphoristically in Fanon's earliest writing is still significant. When the orange-suited detainees were clustered in their Caribbean cages and the naked, bloodied bodies piled up to be categorised and photographed in Abu Ghraib, Bagram, and Diego Garcia according to the specifications of manuals like Raphael Patai's *The Arab Mind*,[30] it became easier to see what Fanon meant by developing the proposition that it is the racist who *produces* the infra-human object as a racialised being.

As he moved from a theory based around the social relations in Martinique toward another approach reoriented by the war in Algeria, Fanon once again confirmed his liberating distance from contemporary debates. He suggested that black and colonised people could damage each other in addition to *and* as a result of the damage done to them by the effects of racial hierarchy. It should not be necessary to emphasise that for him these were not conservative arguments. They were revolutionary sentiments which delivered his readers immediately to the fluid core of his impatient desire for a better, freer, and more dynamically human world than the alienated one for which, in spite of the wounds wrought by colonial rule and its racial hierarchy, he urged us to assume a joint responsibility.

Fanon's theory of liberation was a complex project that drew its intellectual resolution from Marx and Nietzsche, from surrealism, phenomenology, and existentialism, as well as from critical reactions against the narrowness and racism of his postwar training in psychiatry. The resulting mixture was infused with the anger and the political aspirations that he had discovered while serving in the French army and then refined through reading cosmopolitan African American thinkers like Richard Wright. It cannot be divided tidily into early and late versions or split neatly along the axes of existentialism and revolutionary humanism.

The overwhelming desire for national liberation remains constant beneath Fanon's fluctuating attachment to that decidedly nonliberal humanism. Its presence confirms that he was a warrior as well as a healer. Indeed, his political morality can be defined by the urgent obligation to adapt the anti-Nazi commitment for which he was decorated on the battlefield during World War II into an antiracist ethic that could orient the emancipatory goals of the decolonisation struggle. That work can contribute now to the defence of multiculture inside postcolonial Europe.

Fanon's understanding of the necessary place of violence in the brutal passage out of colonial rule has proved to be a perennial issue for commentators on his work. It is much less common to note that his view of its role in securing decolonisation was always tempered by a sophisticated, forensic grasp of the grave psychological and political costs involved for all parties. The warrior's outlook was altered by being combined with the different ethics of a hopeful healer who had learned his trade ministering to the interlocking psychological injuries of the torturer and the tortured. A novel variety of "double consciousness," which pitted an alienated and racialised subject against an emergent human one, affected Fanon's thought in numerous ways. He was stubborn in his faith that reason, science, technology were straightforward instruments of human fulfillment. Racism was bad partly because it perverted those practices and diverted them into unproductive fascination with the trivia of raciology.

The bones of Fanon's first book, *Black Skin, White Masks,* have been picked clean by his scholastic readers. His later essays like "West Indians and Africans" and "Racism and Culture" have received only intermittent attention, even though they present elaborate and nuanced statements of his political thinking at its most iconoclastic and creative. Those writings fill out their author's unshakable commitment to the revolutionary curiosity which had been announced at the end of his first book. His concept of sociogeny, which remains untouched amidst the leftovers of the academic feast, gets elaborated in those essays and provides concrete, practical underpinning for his historical examples. The idea of racism's sociogenesis should refer discussion to the dimensions of raciality that are not economic or political in origin, even if they do become articulated together with economic relations and governmental institutions. Fanon suggests that racial difference has acquired specific capacities in the distinctive social and cultural relations of colonial society that have endured into the present. Yet his subtle use of the "sociogeny" concept suggests a more general applicability. Today it helps us to interpret the patterns of alienation which produce races and racial identification, as well as to isolate the disturbing appearance of the "Negro" as a timely creation that was bound not only to colonial domination but to the global reach of U.S. culture in its mid twentieth-century phase.

That outflow from the United States is now associated with a wide range of cultural changes in which the previously abject and infra-human Negro acquired a peculiar super-human counterpart in the glamorous figure of the black athlete. Understanding that development as sociogeny prompts another disturbing possibility—namely, that the Negro is always a phantom. It corresponds to the historical circumstances in which it appears and is then picked up, acted on, internalised, and fleshed out, with disastrous consequences for all stakeholders in these inglorious transactions. This approach goes some distance beyond simple accounts of racial categories as historical and cultural constructions. In other words, Fanon moved the discussion of race and identity towards what can now be recognised as a *dynamic* nominalism.[31]

Fanon's most significant contribution may be the way that his essays offer powerful protocols for the development of antiracism as a systematic interventionist practice. Here again there are important lessons for contemporary political life. Antiracism is no longer what it was for him—a minor element in a larger theory of revolutionary political agency. In the years since his untimely death, it has become something of a political movement towards equality in its own right. There are several aspects that distinguish his approach to it. First, he puts the global

"South" right back into the centre of accounts of the Cold War. Second, he is alert to the agency of racism in moulding social and political life in the colonies *and* in the metropoles. Most important, he shows that if antiracism is to be politically effective and morally compelling, it must do more than simply imagine that bad ideas can be pumped out of human consciousness and replaced by better ones, while the intractable architecture of racial difference is left intact. In other words, he grasps the full depth and forbidding complexity of the *cultural* dimensions to both colonial and postcolonial conflicts.

His alternative to the trivial approaches characteristic of the era of "identity politics" is spelled out in the essay "Racism and Culture." Some curious and disalienated humans have had their amputated being restored to them. That premature gift has given them a new mission: the pursuit of national liberation. This project proceeds hand in hand with the acquisition of an undreamed-of human liberation, which is more than either an escape from exploitation or the acquisition of autonomy. They are charged with building new forms of solidarity capable of undoing colonial, and by implication postcolonial, rule. Universality, he concludes, "resides in this decision to recognize and accept the reciprocal relativism of different cultures, once the colonial status is irreversibly excluded."[32]

Fanon's life and writings represent an exhortation to join that struggle, which continues in the era of "extraordinary rendition." His insights are all the more precious now that work inside the academy has become so timid and scholastic. The goals of antiracism have been defeated, or perhaps more accurately undone, by strong theories of culture and identity and other race-friendly ideas which have been exported from U.S. history and culture. Those approaches often function as a kind of common sense or default for theoretical discussions of race conducted elsewhere. It is not just that generic versions of blackness and whiteness are being projected globally. A distinctive U.S. racial discourse is offered as the best way to understand and manage racialised politics. In other words, the United States, the world's principal example of successful settler colonialism, has provided foundational norms for discussion of the perils of cultural heterogeneity and the negative impacts of diversity and immigration. U.S. history and political culture have been used to generate ideal types that indicate the future for everybody else on earth when it comes to "race" and racism. U.S.-derived models are advanced as if they reveal a desirable balance between discretely separable civic and ethnic versions of nationalism. U.S. racial technologies are offered as ready-made solutions to the economic and political problems which, we are told, arise from racial division and ethnic plurality.[33]

The fact that racial hierarchy underpins the segregated social and spatial order of the United States is viewed either as an accident or an unfortunate event: either a natural outcome or the result of irresistible market pressures. Condoleezza Rice has followed Francis Fukuyama in describing racism as their country's "birth defect"—a metaphor that suggests it was an outcome of the nation's establishment, rather than its precondition.[34] Their common inattention to the history of U.S. racism and racial hierarchy cements the appeal of *cultural* divisions as a privileged explanation of local, national, and geo-political conflicts. The temptation to indulge in this simplistic variety of analysis has paralleled the rise of securitocracy during the period since the clash of civilisations was projected as an interpretive framework capable of connecting the riots around Paris, the murder of Theo Van Gogh, the Danish cartoon provocations, and the wars in Iraq and Afghanistan.

How we respond to these conditions depends upon how we interpret the confluence of culture talk with civilisationism; how we evaluate the patterns of cultural influence, combination, and conflict that are all around us; and how we understand the significance of the premium that is being placed upon cultural integration and national sameness by European states for whom aspects of U.S. policy in this field have acquired great appeal.

Another, better theory of cultural plurality is needed—but that is not being proposed here. It seems more important to try to generate histories of multiculture that are alive to the power of the colonial past, yet sensitive to the convivial, social interaction practised ordinarily and routinely in the everyday life of multicultural and postcolonial cities. Analysis of that conviviality shifts the focus of enquiry away from the *cultural* resources that precede interactive events and transcultural contacts. Attention gets directed instead towards the habitual pleasures of cosmopolitan interaction and the basic fact of interdependency. The conflicts generated and the care that can arise destabilise the notion that we are dealing with discrete racial or *ethnic* enclaves made material in urban form. This unruly world is too chaotic to be represented as a mosaic of cultural fragments that could be arranged into a nation-centred picture puzzle. We discover dizzying patterns of desire, translation, and transcultural imagination that attend conviviality's economic aspects and inform its vernacular sociality.[35] Even if convivial contact can be rearticulated as a form of solidarity bounded by class feeling or locality, interaction across what we are often wrongly told are impermeable cultural lines should be recognised as dynamically productive.

It bears repeating that opportunities to expand and fulfill democracy have emerged when racism and ethnic absolutism are identified as problems amenable to political action and, even temporarily, overcome. The refusal of racialised hierarchy and marginality is itself a civic asset which can deepen political life and enhance the fragile, universal humanity to which rights are addressed and attached. It is possible, too, that convivial contact across culture lines will augment the economic networks found even in the poorest and most conflict-ridden communities and create or promote awareness of interdependency, relationality, and shared or common fate. Art itself and its multicultural institutions can play a role in promoting conversation, translation, and cosmopolitan recognition that contrast sharply with the civilisationist tendency to misrecognise culture and approach it as if it could be absolute property.

These conflicts over culture do more than supply the ground upon which the problems of security in the overdeveloped countries will be settled. They correspond to the residual effects of lost imperial power, and they carry other lessons. They suggest that Europe should not continue to import U.S.-oriented conceptions of ethno-racial difference, or to use the history of the United States in order to sustain the idea that solidarity and diversity are essentially incompatible, particularly in the context of welfare state provision. With racism placed at the centre of analysis, we can also see that the United States is not in advance of Europe on some grand, teleological journey towards the successful management of minorities and alien incomers and the orchestration of their smooth, involutionary transformation into uniform citizens.

Since September 2001, the overamplified rhetoric of civilisationism has taken hold of U.S. geo-political pronouncements. The pursuit of an impossible invulnerability seems to have determined many strategic choices. Those developments have also affected the cultural conflicts that are now integral to the exercise of U.S. power and to the various forms of resistance against it in the era of Facebook diplomacy, To the Fallen Records, and TroopTube.tv.

The U.S. military now represents its nation's diversity and cultural plurality more comprehensively than any other institution. This point can be underscored by introducing the figures of Shoshana Johnson and the late Lori Ann Piestewa, soldiers who fought alongside their better-known comrade in arms, Jessica Lynch, during the invasion of Iraq. The fact that they were, respectively, African and Native American proved no obstacle to their full participation in that imperial adventure. Johnson, a cook who became the U.S. military's first black female POW, did not enjoy the same post-battlefield celebrity as her colleague and friend. Though they shared a well-publicised opportunity to meet Britney Spears, instead of a million-dollar book deal Johnson got to hang out with Queen Latifah and drop the ball in the 2003 New Year's Eve celebrations in Times Square. Piestewa, a twenty-four-year-old Hopi mother of two from a family with several generations of military service, was the first Native American woman to be killed in action fighting for the United States; she died in an ambush during the early days of the Iraq War, in March 2005, and was posthumously awarded a Purple Heart and a promotion. During the spring of 2005, Jessica Lynch, who has consistently sought to honour her dead comrade, was featured on the reality TV show *Extreme Makeover: Home Edition*. She was part of a team that erected a new house for Piestewa's parents and her children. What kind of measure of America's racial nomos do these discrepancies suggest? Was a degree of conviviality produced by the humanising powers of class and gender solidarity, interdependence, and ordinary transcultural contact perhaps evident among these American women in the multicultural belly of the military beast?

The Cultural Counterpart to "Kinetic War"

The latest neo-imperial belligerence has been underpinned by a crude political theology that should be familiar to analysts of colonial history. It is now articulated with a U.S. nationalism that is as pious as it is brittle, exceptionalist, and belligerent. The ideas of race and culture fuse and create a fundamental index of civilisational difference that cannot be denatured. A duplicitous, embedded anthropology solidifies mere cultural contrasts. It promotes their transformation into metaphysical differences that can fuel and justify the tactical calculations of emboldened statecraft. An equally unbridgeable division, this time between friends and enemies, has altered the pattern of cultural relationships between the West and the rest of the world. These changes have militarised government and everyday life in many places and transformed understanding of the emergent cultural and political forms of globalisation which appear now primarily as securitocracy.

The inescapable fate of the overdeveloped countries is being regularly and repeatedly specified as an endless or, more recently, just a long counter-insurgency war. That protracted conflict is to be waged against a constantly shifting group of targets: failed or recalcitrant states and nonstate actors, as well as ideas, ideologies, dispositions, and various cultural pathologies that attend the wretched lives of the barbarous and implicitly infra-human peoples who hate our freedoms and way of life. Undoing and changing those hostile cultures demands new patterns of cultural intervention based upon new technologies and associated with new varieties of diplomacy. This was explained carefully in the 2005 report of the U.S. State Department's Advisory Committee on Cultural Diplomacy:

> Cultural diplomacy is the linchpin of public diplomacy; for it is in cultural activities that a nation's idea of itself is best represented. And cultural diplomacy can enhance our national security in subtle, wide-ranging, and sustainable ways. Indeed history may record that America's cultural riches played no less a role than military action in shaping our international leadership, including the war on terror. For the values embedded in our artistic and intellectual traditions form a bulwark against the forces of darkness.[36]

A second stated goal of these new strategic developments was to combat the idea that Americans are "shallow, violent and godless." But these initiatives have not been matched by any growth in the moral authority of the United States. Instead, the country's foreign policy has continued to polarise global opinion, giving shape and purpose to an increasing ambivalence about its economic, cultural, and military domination of the world. Poll data about the way that the United States is seen from the outside shows that the proportion of distrustful and negative views varies from country to country and can be highly contradictory in character,[37] but it is clear that the country is not winning the global struggle for hearts and minds. The popular idea that individual success can be measured by the goal of becoming American, or perhaps more realistically by the prospect of migrating to the United States, still retains wide-spread appeal. Yet even after the election of Barack Obama,[38] the country has lost much of the unique appeal invested in it by its economic and military preeminence and by its control of the "infotainment telesector."[39] Notwithstanding that dreamscape, the U.S. government is likely these days to be seen instead as decadent, bullying, and unjust both in its dealings with its own citizens and in its apparently authoritarian attempts to direct world economics and politics in its own interest.

The proliferation of states of exception and emergency means that inside the fortified homelands of affluence, citizenship is no longer what it was. Its residual protections are unevenly distributed, and they remain sharply qualified by growing inequality as well as by a de facto racial hierarchy buried inside simplistic accounts of the difference faith makes. The tension between hyperbolic pronouncements about freedom and democracy and the sternly segregated reality of U.S. society not only provides a framework through which these injustices are perceived, but has also helped to nurture a global public sphere by transmitting any internal dissent outwards to a transnational public.

Before we get carried away by the promise of transnational political communities, we should remember that a sizable majority of people on our planet have never heard a telephone dialtone. The information technology that facilitates and prefigures global networks is still heavily concentrated in the overdeveloped zones. Yet a nascent global immanence[40] conditions the larger setting in which the political dynamics of U.S. culture is being recast and contested. The manifestation of these new geo-political and geo-cultural arrangements has done more than simply alter the balance previously struck between "hard" and "soft" forms of power. Qualitative changes have occurred in the way that power is conceived and exercised.

This is the setting in which rock and roll has become just another weapon on the battlefield and an instrument of, or an accompaniment to, torture.[41] Hip hop and rhythm and blues have been directly co-opted into the machinations of the war effort from above and from below. Troops involved in the April 2004 siege of Fallujah were reported to be incorporating Hendrix's music—alongside that of AC/DC—into their battlefield tactics.[42] The 2009 release of rapper 50 Cent's video game "50 Cent: Blood on the Sand" exclusively featured a number of new tracks. It is set in Iraq, where he battles Al-Qaeda in order to recover his stolen gold jewelry. The acts of "gangsta" rebellion and resistance that confirmed his status as both "Nigga" and bankable commodity have been made official and then co-opted into the digital struggle for hearts and minds at home and abroad.

This situation demands new tools for understanding the relationship between racial hierarchy and nationalism, as well as a more elaborate analysis of the dynamics of political culture transformed by technology, info-war, and the development of public diplomacy.[43] Some aspects of this shift were foreshadowed in the writings of twentieth-century analysts of propaganda, truth, media, and government such as Freud, Orwell, and Bernays.[44] But their approach seems blunt when it is addressed to the complexities of today's hi-tech global media manipulation. Military initiatives are no longer conceptualised as punctuated, complemented, and facilitated by psychological operations ("psy-ops") that were essentially external to them. The character of this new variety of war—and the absolutely secure forms of social life that correspond to it—require the wholesale integration of struggles over information, language, and symbols with the prosecution of the conflict itself. In Afghanistan, anthropologists are embedded among the troops on low-intensity battlefields, while nominally independent NGOs support the NATO war effort by providing Afghan citizens with mobile phones—the preferred means to combat the viral circulation of "antiwestern" clips among the country's half-million Internet users and estimated six million mobile-phone owners.[45] These conditions reveal how hard and soft power are effectively fused, and how securitocracy requires that each dimension of power take on characteristics and tactical significance associated with the other. What Edward Bernays described long ago as the "engineering of consent" now operates on a number of scales and saturates the workings of the twenty-four-hour media environment, orchestrating ignorance and diverting healthy curiosity into uncontroversial or marginal directions. Any democratic potential inherent in increasing the flow of information is itself circumscribed by the role of governmental and media institutions in the systematic cultural production of ignorance.[46] Something like Walter Benjamin's aestheticisation of politics combines seamlessly with an anaesthetic parapolitics. That combination requires a revised account of the relationships between ignorance, knowledge, and governmental power.

These changes are not reducible to the effects of technology alone. The dissemination of the photographic archive of U.S. prisoner abuse at Abu Ghraib can be cited to illustrate many of the fundamental mechanisms involved in the viral circulation and dissemination of digital fragments, but the bulk of those images have never been publicly displayed. Digital still photography is already an anachronistic vector in this global contest of images, symbols, and icons. The period after Major General Geoffrey Miller's epoch-making transfer to Iraq to secure the Gitmo-isation of the U.S. prison regime there was characterised by a quantum leap in video-blogging, uploading, and self-documentation that has defied military "emissions control" and expanded immediate public access to the experiential and political detail of the war. The integrity of that free communicative space seems now to be essential to the morale of the occupying forces. The military authorities have worked hard to restrict and confine their personnel's access to approved and filtered channels of digital communication.[47]

The circulation of material of that sort does not guarantee any particular political result. It is now part of a mainstream culture of uploading and self-display that threatens to decentre the geo-politics of information and rework the patterns of distribution beyond the point where they can be effectively orchestrated by any national state or corporate entity. This helps to explain how, even in a "unipolar" world, the brand value and identity of the United States appear to be so swiftly and openly at stake in the conduct of its military operations. It cannot be said too often that African American culture now contributes directly to that value and to the geo-political interests of the nation. It, too, should be considered a weapon in the increasingly important arsenal of U.S. cultural power. In a polemic in favour of a thoughtful, hi-tech engagement with the teenagers of the Middle East—who, it turns out, are just like American teenagers—Jared Cohen, who was responsible for counterterrorism, counter-radicalisation, youth and education, public diplomacy, Muslim world outreach, and the Maghreb under Condoleezza Rice in the State Department, described the current situation like this:

> While young and old alike use and enjoy satellite television, radio, Internet, and mobile phones, the generations are using them in completely different ways. For young people, technology is first and foremost a means to express themselves, interact, generate their own media and shape a digital identity that may or may not be in sync with real life. . . . The youth are not only using technology to communicate with one another; they are using it to communicate with the rest of the world. . . . The language they speak is not exclusively the language of politics. Instead, it is about a common set of norms and values that are characteristic of young people around the world.[48]

Many dimensions of this novel technological and cultural environment merit detailed investigation. Yet the questions of racial hierarchy and injustice that have loomed large within it are seldom addressed directly, and are rarely recognised as a significant element in how broad judgements of the United States are being formed and how the country's cultural resources—including the lingua franca of global youth—are to be understood. The issues which did so much to compromise the demo-

cratic integrity of the United States during the embittered era of civil
rights struggles have acquired a new significance in the postcolonial
world, where representations of multiculture and diversity have acquired a high market value, even if politicians and governments find
them difficult to imagine, to appreciate, and to manipulate.

The disjunction between formal adherence to cultural diversity and
the prosecution of imperial adventures was first brought home by the
strange situation in which the camps at Guantánamo Bay, like detention
facilities run elsewhere by the United States, could boast of feeding their
detainees "culturally appropriate meals" while simultaneously using the
very same knowledge of cultural differences to perpetrate specific forms
of humiliation and abuse. James Yee, formerly the U.S. Military Imam at
the Cuban base, has described the desecration of religious texts and the
use of culturally inappropriate gender behaviour as a recurrent part of
the interrogation process.[49] Janis Karpinski, the Arabic-speaking former general who had been in charge of the Abu Ghraib facility before
Miller took over, has claimed with the greatest sincerity that reading the
Koran had "enhanced" her own spirituality.[50] These illustrations should
not be dismissed as the institutional consequences of a "politically correct" corporate management culture. They provide small yet valuable
portals through which we can consider the day-to-day functioning of
the U.S. version of managed diversity that is being exported to the rest
of the world. A formal, anodyne multiculturalism is part of the racial
technology embedded in the conduct of the "war on terror," understood
now as a *global* insurgency.[51]

Much of what now passes for U.S. culture worldwide is in fact African
American in either character or derivation. Contemporary reflections
on the question of racism and its relationship to multiculture, rights,
opportunity, and democracy arise under the symbolic umbrella spec-
tacularly provided by the pivotal, historic personality of President
Obama. Like Rice before him, he is a timely and welcome embodiment
of U.S. success in extending political rights and educational opportuni-

ties to a privileged caste drawn from racial and ethnic minorities. He provides a smiling human cipher for the national-security strategy and presents the official face of U.S. diversity, united across racial lines by a fundamental patriotic commitment to the advancement of national interests. Rice's polished aura added something distinctive to the political visibility of the United States in the world. The epiphany represented by President Obama should also offer an immediate and vivid lesson about the irrelevance of race to the operations of government. Yet—again like Rice—his studied celebrity is often deployed either to convey the contentious proposition that racism has now been dealt with and equality of opportunity finally secured, or to raise unanswerable questions about the nature of racial authenticity.[52]

The political debates over racism and ethnicity that have emerged in response to Rice's power and Obama's presidential presence have been raised by critical considerations of the legal and humanitarian conduct of the war against terrorism. Pertinent questions have been asked about the issue of U.S. war crimes, about the routine practice of torture, and about the habitual use of extrajudicial detention, all of which seem to be continuous with older forms of colonial warfare driven by orientalist, civilisationist, and racialist conceptions of human hierarchy and history.[53]

Similar themes have been debated with great intensity since the pursuit of rights and recognition by the country's substantial Hispanic minorities resulted in mass demonstrations of their centrality and value within the U.S. economy. That development also prompted important reflections on the history and memory of the twentieth-century civil rights movement by African Americans, at a moment when they were no longer their country's largest "nonwhite" group and have been struggling to come to terms with the fact that their distinctive cultural habits and styles have been more comprehensively mainstreamed than ever before without yielding any discernible benefit to the vast majority of African Americans.[54]

The expansion of hip hop into something like the official communicative idiom of an increasingly globalised youth culture that is judged vulnerable to the seductions of political Islam has had important unanticipated effects. Numerous soldiers on the frontline of U.S. military operations have opted to articulate their disenchantment and their resignation in the form of rap performances which they have recorded, edited for circulation, and combined with their own video footage. Rather than consume a soundtrack for their experience devised elsewhere and then sold back to them as a finished commodity—Beyoncé's 2005 hit "Soldier" was a good example of that corporate dynamic—they have acquired the tools not only to produce their own alternative musical accompaniment, but to distribute it worldwide as well.[55] The same is true of their opponents, who have uploaded videos of their own insurgent exploits—sometimes choreographed to peculiarly inappropriate U.S. musical soundtracks.

That is the contradiction into which the tentacles of anthropologically literate and resolutely hi-tech cultural and public diplomacy are being extended. Though mainstream black culture's interfacing with endless war should not be used to dismiss hip hop as a whole, it reveals something profound about the changing character of U.S. society and about the country's evolution towards a new racial settlement in which corporate multiculturalism can coexist comfortably with mass incarceration and growing inequality. Under the aegis of corporate powers like the Hummer Corporation, MTV, and BET, these unlikely connections have been essential to the process of military recruitment for some time.[56] What is at issue now is whether the United States's strong attachment to and persistent celebration of its distinctive conception of racial hierarchy will prove an obstacle to the continued export and circulation of its exhilarating cultural products.

Many people outside the country will never share its peculiar appetite for seeing reality-TV contestants divided into race-specific teams, or having DNA analysed according to the local rules of "phenomics" in order to establish the probity of a particular racial heritage.[57] However much they enjoy the brand-saturated pleasures of Hollywood, hip hop, McDonalds, SUVs, and African American style, the question is now whether U.S. attachment to the idea of race retains the power to detonate the unstable reconciliation of its hard and soft powers deployed in a global counter-insurgency.

My cherished hope is that rather than choose to remain within that hall of distorting mirrors, the rest of the world will be able to move towards a renunciation of the foundational absurdities of U.S. race talk. In opting for the former and following what I see as the more cautious, conservative path, we would be deciding to repeat the drama of Fanon's famous primal scene. It involved, you may recall, the figure of a deeply ambivalent postcolonial immigrant who sees himself being seen and feels the impact of being captured by the spectatorship of white onlookers, who freely amputate his humanity and reduce him to the status of an alienated, infra-human object among other objects. In the street, or perhaps on public transport, those observers perceive nothing in his apologetic presence save the unchanging dimensions of an ineffable, threatening otherness.

I do not think we should play down the significance of those encounters. But before we decide, overdefensively, to replay that scene indefinitely and make it the tacit premise of an antiracist politics that cannot say what we favour as easily as what we oppose, we should remember that the imperial potency of the north Atlantic is now in irreversible decline. On the edge of a new epoch in which U.S. diversity management has begun to look unconvincing if not irrelevant in the face of economic upheaval and geo-political conflict, we can begin to inquire into the possibility of moving beyond and beneath the old colonial dramaturgy into a more forward-looking and assertively cosmopolitan stance that requires a new history of the postcolonial present bolstered by some equally novel ways of comprehending and figuring our vulnerable humanity.

There are precious narratives of liberation from white supremacy and the pursuit of equality to be gleaned from elsewhere. Conviviality and multiculture can be found on our own doorsteps. There are accounts of the movements against slavery, colonialism, and imperial rule that were not centred in the U.S. racial nomos. The histories of South Africa, India, and Brazil will all contribute abundantly to a deprovincialising reassessment and reconstruction. An antiracist political imaginary will build communicative networks that facilitate a different variety of worldly conversation on these matters.

In conclusion, I am prepared to concede that there may still be things to learn from the U.S. acceptance of "race," providing that it is accompanied by an acknowledgement of the damage done by racism and does not become a blank resignation to the effects of racial hierarchy. Yet my essential point remains: accepting the salience of the social and political processes that the United States knows and sees as a natural phenomenon called "race" does absolutely nothing to address the multiple mystifications wrought by racism, either in U.S. political culture or elsewhere.

Deciding whether the precious gift of African American freedom struggles is something others can still adapt has simply become a secondary issue. Their world-historic culture of freedom has lost its purchase on events and been overtaken by what appears to be its successor: a celebration of limitless consumer freedoms that is as unsustainable as it is immoral.

The legacy of Douglass, Du Bois, Wells, Phyllis Wheatley, and Beecher Stowe has been reworked and its traditions reconfigured to fit newer assumptions about what it means to be seen to be free. Yet the vestiges of that historic formation can now be claimed by more than narrowly national interests. They might even be recovered in ways that enhance a cosmopolitan view of where struggles against racial hierarchy can deepen and democratise humankind in our transition out of the neoliberal order.

The balance between audio and video has been transformed from the days of Alain Locke's troubadours, but the machinery of infowar and the new cultural diplomacy are still forced to make use of music, and that may yet prove their undoing. Jimi, Curtis, and the antiwar movement to which they were committed cannot, of course, furnish us with an anticipatory practice of freedom addressed to our own time. Their fading example cannot compete with digital consumerism or answer digital imperialism. Nonetheless, the ideas of peace, love, and harmony with nature that characterised their perilous time are still reminders of where important resources of hope might be located. Perhaps the most precious and sustaining varieties of hope reside in a relationship between music and peace which is deeper than the ones that games consoles and MP3s can accommodate. This yet-to-come might be awakened by our renewed commitment to the ancient idea that listening and dancing together helps us to break through and out of a world of reified relationships. The music hits you, and you feel no pain. There will be a new Earth. The contorted, pitchless screams of discontent that elevated Hendrix's "Machine Gun" still point to that verdict, even here, even now.

Notes

1. Get Free or Die Tryin'

1. E. Franklin Frazier, *Black Bourgeoisie* (New York: Collier, 1966; orig. pub. 1957).

2. Victoria de Grazia, *Irresistible Empire: America's Advance Through Twentieth-Century Europe* (Cambridge, Mass.: Harvard University Press, 2005).

3. E. P. Thompson, "The Moral Economy of the English Crowd during the Eighteenth Century," in Thompson, *Customs in Common* (New York: Penguin, 1993). Thompson's essay was written in 1963 and originally published in 1971. In a later essay that revisited the work, he explained its distinctive conceptual and "methodological" orientation towards "particular market-places and particular practices in dealing" (Thompson, "Moral Economy Reviewed," ibid., 261).

4. Benjamin R. Barber, *Consumed: How Markets Corrupt Children, Infantilize Adults, and Swallow Citizens Whole* (New York: Norton, 2008).

5. Kenneth W. Goings, *Mammy and Uncle Mose: Black Collectibles and American Stereotyping* (Bloomington: Indiana University Press, 1994); Jackie Young, *Black Collectables: Mammy and Her Friends* (West Chester, Pa.:

Schiffer, 1988); Patricia Turner, *Ceramic Uncles and Celluloid Mammies: Black Images and Their Influence on Culture* (Charlottesville: University of Virginia Press, 2002).

6. Marilyn Halter, *Shopping for Identity: The Marketing of Ethnicity* (New York: Schocken, 2000).

7. Shane White and Graham White, *Stylin' African American Expressive Culture* (Ithaca, N.Y.: Cornell University Press, 1998).

8. Frantz Fanon, *Black Skin, White Masks,* trans. Charles Lam Marckmann (London: Pluto, 1986; orig. French ed. 1952), 109.

9. Barbara Keys, "Spreading Peace, Democracy and Coca Cola: Sport and American Cultural Expansion in the 1930s," *Diplomatic History,* 28, no. 2 (April 2004): 165–196.

10. Henry Ford's involvement in and promotion of fiddling is typical of the developments that I have in mind here. See Charles Wolfe, *The Devil's Box: Masters of Southern Fiddling* (Nashville: Vanderbilt University Press / Country Music Foundation, 1997).

11. Edward L. Bernays, ed., *The Engineering of Consent* (Norman: University of Oklahoma Press, 1955; orig. pub. 1947).

12. Paul K. Edwards, *The Southern Urban Negro as a Consumer* (New York: Prentice-Hall, 1932).

13. Henry Allen Bullock, "Consumer Motivations in Black and White," *Harvard Business Review,* 39, no. 3 (May–June 1961): 93.

14. George Joyce and Norman A. P. Govoni, *The Black Consumer: Dimensions of Behavior and Strategy* (New York: Random House, 1971).

15. Fanon, *Black Skin, White Masks,* 112.

16. Martin Luther King Jr., *Stride toward Freedom: The Montgomery Story* (London: Gollancz, 1959), 70.

17. Kristin Ross, *Fast Cars, Clean Bodies: Decolonization and the Reordering of French Culture* (Cambridge, Mass.: MIT Press, 1995), 19. See also Terry Smith, *Making the Modern: Industry, Art and Design in America* (Chicago: University of Chicago Press, 1993), esp. part 1.

18. "From the beginning, Americans used automobile ownership, especially of large, powerful automobiles, in a quest for respect." Tom McCarthy, *Auto Mania: Cars, Consumers, and the Environment* (New Haven, Conn.: Yale University Press, 2007), 29.

19. See Kathleen Franz, "'The Open Road': Automobility and Racial Uplift in the Interwar Years," in Bruce Sinclair, ed., *Technology and the African American Experience* (Cambridge, Mass.: MIT Press, 2004).

20. James S. Duesenberry, *Income, Saving and the Theory of Consumer Behavior* (Cambridge, Mass.: Harvard University Press, 1949); Robert Weems, "The Revolution Will Be Marketed: American Corporations and Black Consumers during the 1960s," *Radical History Review*, 59 (1994): 94–107; Virág Molnár and Michèle Lamont, "Social Categorization and Group Identification: How African-Americans Shape Their Collective Identity through Consumption," in Kenneth Green et al., eds., *Interdisciplinary Approaches to Demand and Its Role in Innovation* (Manchester, U.K.: Manchester University Press, forthcoming).

21. Steve Nadis and James J. MacKenzie, *Car Trouble* (Boston: Beacon, 1993); and Jane Holtz Kay, *Asphalt Nation: How the Automobile Took Over America, and How We Can Take It Back* (Berkeley: University of California Press, 1997). See also the car pages of Melanet, at melanet.com.

22. I must thank Radiclani Clytus for the information that the term "whips" seems to be an abbreviation of "whip 'n' ride" or "whippin' ride."

23. "When Buick wanted to increase sales of its luxury Park Avenue model to minority buyers, it noticed that African Americans frequently have lower rates of home ownership but more disposable cash than whites at similar income levels. Affluent African Americans, the company discovered, were being ignored as potential Park Avenue purchasers simply because their status as renters didn't fit the traditional buyer profile. . . . 'A lot of companies pay lip service to targeting minority groups,' says Patrick Harrison, marketing line manager at Buick. 'But we wanted our Buick dealers to develop a personal relationship with African Americans. And this is how we found a way to bring minorities into our dealerships.'" Michael J. Weiss, *The Clustered World: How We Live, What We Buy, and What It All Means about Who We Are* (Boston: Little, Brown, 2000), 96–97.

24. www.census.gov/hhes/www/wealth/1998_2000/wlth00–5.html (accessed April 24, 2009).

25. Ralph Ellison, "Cadillac Flambé," *American Review*, 16 (February 1973): 249–269.

26. The story is reprinted in *Callaloo,* 18, no. 4 (Spring 1995): 251–262 (quotation on 257).

27. T. W. Adorno, "More Haste, Less Speed," in Adorno, *Minima Moralia,* trans. E. F. N. Jephcott (London: Verso, 1974), 102.

28. Wolfgang Sachs, *For the Love of the Automobile,* trans. Don Reneau (Berkeley: University of California Press, 1992).

29. W. E. B. Du Bois, "Close Ranks," in *The Crisis,* 16 (July 1918).

30. Loic Wacquant, "Deadly Symbiosis: When Ghetto and Prison Meet and Mesh," *Punishment and Society,* 3, no. 1 (2001): 95–133.

31. Black America's distinguished public intellectual Cornel West conceded this much when, in the opening pages of his best-selling book *Race Matters* (Boston: Beacon, 1993), he described leaving his "rather elegant" car in a safe parking lot before riding uptown to East Harlem to have his photograph taken. The desire for unobstructed access to Manhattan taxis is a recurrent feature of much of the discourse recently produced to communicate the hurt and injury of U.S. racism. The full ground-shaking force of the primal scene in which taxi travel is denied by the leviathan of white supremacy can be appreciated, I suggest, only in the context of the romance of automotivity. The idea that public transport might provide an alternative never comes into consideration.

32. Raymond Williams, *Towards 2000* (New York: Penguin, 1985), 188.

33. Thomas Freidman, *The Lexus and the Olive Tree: Understanding Globalization* (New York: Anchor, 2000), 464.

34. Jean Baudrillard, *For a Critique of the Political Economy of the Sign,* trans. Charles Levin (St. Louis: Telos, 1981), esp. ch. 7.

35. David E. Nye, *Consuming Power: A Social History of American Energies* (Cambridge, Mass.: MIT Press, 1998), 182.

36. bell hooks, *Wounds of Passion: A Writing Life* (London: Women's Press, 1997), 47.

37. Theodore Rosengarten and Nate Shaw, *All God's Dangers: The Life of Nate Shaw* (New York: Random House, 1974).

38. Houston A. Baker Jr., *Blues, Ideology, and Afro-American Literature: A Vernacular Theory* (Chicago: University of Chicago Press, 1984).

39. W. T. Lhamon Jr., *Deliberate Speed: The Origins of a Cultural Style in the*

American 1950s (Washington, D.C.: Smithsonian Institution Press, 1990), 78–86.

40. The "alley" was, for example, no longer a place of play and self-discovery.

41. Susan Strasser, *Waste and Want: A Social History of Trash* (New York: Metropolitan Books, 1999), p. 192.

42. See www.strategicvision.com/pdf/auto_2007_ethnic_release.pdf (accessed May 22, 2009).

43. Juliet Schor, *The Overspent American: Upscaling, Downshifting, and the New Consumer* (New York: Basic Books, 1998).

44. Clay McShane, *Down the Asphalt Path: The Automobile and the American City* (New York: Columbia University Press, 1994), ch. 6.

45. Ibid., 122.

46. David E. Nye, *Consuming Power: A Social History of American Energies* (Cambridge, Mass.: MIT Press, 1998), 178.

47. Walter LaFeber, *Michael Jordan and the New Global Capitalism* (New York: Norton, 1999).

48. Gail Bederman, *Manliness and Civilization: A Cultural History of Gender and Race in the United States, 1880–1917* (Chicago: University of Chicago Press, 1995).

49. Randy Roberts, *Papa Jack: Jack Johnson and the Era of White Hopes* (London: Robson, 1983), 120.

50. McShane, *Down the Asphalt Path*, 134.

51. See, for example, aacardealers.org (accessed May 22, 2009). The site offers "a history of the pioneering African-American men and women who elected to pursue a business career as franchised new car dealers within the automotive industry." An African American car-buyers' guide (aacbg.com, accessed May 22, 2009) was put together under the aegis of Melanet, the "uncut black experience on the internet." See also August Meier and Elliott Rudwick, *Black Detroit and the Rise of the UAW* (New York: Oxford University Press, 1979); and James J. Flink, *The Automobile Age* (Cambridge, Mass.: MIT Press, 1990), esp. 126–128.

52. James Flink, who has coined the useful concept of "automobility," addresses these issues with great insight. "In the black ghetto of Inkster,

Michigan, adjacent to lily-white Dearborn, a bastion of the Ku Klux Klan, Ford set up a gigantic plantation for his black workers. He paid them only $1 a day in cash of their $4 wage, the remaining $3 in food and clothing from a public commissary. Seeds to plant in garden patches and communal sowing machines were also furnished to Ford's Inkster blacks (Flink, *The Automobile Age,* 221).

53. Henry Ford, *The International Jew: The World's Foremost Problem* (Honolulu: University Press of the Pacific, 2003); Adolf Hitler, *Mein Kampf,* trans. Ralph Manheim (Boston: Houghton Mifflin, 1943), 639. On Ford and Hitler, see Charles Higham, *Trading with the Enemy: An Exposé of the Nazi-American Money Plot, 1933–1949* (New York: Delacorte, 1983). "Trusteeship": Ken Silverstein, "Ford and the Führer: New Documents Reveal Close Ties between Dearborn and the Nazis," *The Nation,* 270, no. 3 (January 2000): 11–18.

54. Dennis Wepman et al., comps., *The Life: The Lore and Folk Poetry of the Black Hustler* (Philadelphia: University of Pennsylvania Press, 1976), 135; John Lomax and Alan Lomax, comps., *American Ballads and Folk Songs* (New York: Macmillan, 1934).

55. Think, for example, of the lyrics of Marvin Gaye's "Mercy Mercy Me (The Ecology)," from the album *What's Going On?* Or Curtis Mayfield's "Future Shock," from the album *Back to the World.*

56. William DeVaughn, "Be Thankful for What You Got" (Roxbury Records, 1975).

57. Missy Elliott, "The Rain (Supa Dupa Fly)" (East West Records, 1997).

58. Youtube.com/watch?v=5xdBn_mWigY. Cool and Dre, *The Epidemic Begins Now* (Pinnacle Records, 2007).

59. Suzanne E. Smith, *Dancing in the Street: Motown and the Cultural Politics of Detroit* (Cambridge, Mass.: Harvard University Press, 1999).

60. See, for example, aacbg.com. See also Meier and Rudwick, *Black Detroit;* and Flink, *The Automobile Age,* esp. 126–128.

61. Richard Wright, *Native Son* (New York: Harper, 1940), 54.

62. *The Source* (New York), 105 (June 1998): 109.

63. Ibid., 117 (June 1999): 136.

64. Edward Helmore, "No Limit for Master P," *The Observer* (London), 17 October 1999, 7.

65. This according to the memoir by Peter F. Drucker, *Adventures of a Bystander* (New York: Harper and Row, 1979), as quoted in Dan Rose, *Black American Street Life: South Philadelphia, 1969–1971* (Philadelphia: University of Pennsylvania Press, 1987), 104.

66. Peter Hoy, "Hip Hop Hot Rods," *Forbes*, 16 August 2007.

67. *The Source*, 117 (June 1999): 144.

68. Peter Relic, "Big Black Truck: Buckle Up for an Expedition in Montell Jordan's Jiggmobile," *Vibe* (New York), June–July 1998, 117.

69. *Newsweek*, 20 June 2005. See also www.autolinedetroit.tv/show/1234 /extra (accessed May 22, 2009).

2. Declaration of Rights

1. The journal *Human Rights* was a four-page monthly publication favoring immediate abolition. It was edited by the atheist and actuary Elizur Wright, and appeared during the years 1835–1838. Its masthead proclaimed: "Our object is liberty for all, gained by moral power and regulated by impartial laws." *Human Rights*, 1, no. 1 (August 1835). See also Elizur Wright Jr., *The Sin of Slavery and Its Remedy: Containing Some Reflections on the Moral Influence of African Colonization* (New York, 1833), 3: "While this nation held up its declaration of independence—its noble bill of human rights, before an admiring world, in one hand; it mortified the friends of humanity, by oppressing the poor and defenceless with the other. The progress of time has not lessened the evil. There are now held in involuntary and perpetual slavery, in the southern half of this republic, more than 2,000,000 of men, women, and children, guarded with a vigilance, which strives, and with success appalling as it is complete, to shut out every ray of knowledge, human and divine, and reduce them as nearly as possible to a level with the brutes." See also "A Word of Encouragement," *Frederick Douglass' Paper*, February 12, 1852: "Our able Corresponding editor is (as most of our readers know) a white man; many, who contribute to our columns are, also, white persons; and our subscribers are (two-thirds of them) of the favored class. On the other hand, some of the most valuable communications in prose and poetry, found in our columns, are from the pens of colored men. The excellent articles, over the signatures 'Communipaw,' 'S.R.W.,' 'Ethiop,' 'J.C.H.,'

'Cosmopolite,' 'Observer,' 'W.G.A.,' and others, are the productions of the latter class. Here we are then, just as we ought to be, all at work in the great field of thought, battling for the overthrow of slavery, prejudice and national antipathy, and wielding together the long broken links in the chain of human brotherhood. It is not a white man's paper, nor a black man's paper as such; but a paper for UNIVERSAL MAN. True to its comprehensive motto of 'ALL RIGHTS FOR ALL,' we feel confident that its friends will be found among all and its burdens be shared by all."

2. Robert Wedderburn, *The Horrors of Slavery and Other Writings*, ed. Iain McCalman (Edinburgh: Edinburgh University Press, 1991); Harriet Martineau, *The Martyr Age of the United States of America, with an Appeal on Behalf of the Oberlin Institute in Aid of the Abolition of Slavery* (Newcastle on Tyne: Emancipation and Aborigines Protection Society, 1840).

3. George Fredrickson, *Racism: A Short History* (Princeton, N.J.: Princeton University Press, 2002); George L. Mosse, *Toward the Final Solution: A History of European Racism,* 2nd ed. (Madison: University of Wisconsin Press, 1985; orig. pub. 1978).

4. Mahmood Mamdani, ed., *Beyond Rights Talk and Culture Talk: Comparative Essays on the Politics of Rights and Culture* (New York: St. Martin's, 2000).

5. Michael Ignatieff et al., *Human Rights as Politics and Idolatry,* ed. Amy Gutmann (Princeton, N.J.: Princeton University Press, 2001); Michael Ignatieff, *The Rights Revolution* (Toronto: Anansi, 2000); Lynn Hunt, *Inventing Human Rights: A History* (New York: Norton, 2007); Geoffrey Robertson, *Crimes against Humanity: The Struggle for Global Justice* (New York: Penguin, 2000).

6. Enrique Dussel, *The Invention of the Americas: Eclipse of "the Other" and the Myth of Modernity,* trans. Michael D. Barber (New York: Continuum, 1995); idem, *The Underside of Modernity: Apel, Ricoeur, Rorty, Taylor, and the Philosophy of Liberation,* trans. Eduardo Mendieta (Atlantic Highlands, N.J.: Humanities Press, 1996); Tzvetan Todorov, *The Conquest of America: The Question of the Other,* trans. Richard Howard (New York: Harper and Row, 1984); idem, *On Human Diversity: Nationalism, Racism, and Exoticism in*

French Thought, trans. Catherine Porter (Cambridge, Mass.: Harvard University Press, 1993).

7. Peter Hulme, "The Spontaneous Hand of Nature: Savagery, Colonialism and Enlightenment," in Peter Hulme and Ludmilla Jordanova, eds., *The Enlightenment and Its Shadows* (London: Routledge, 1990).

8. Uday Singh Mehta, *Liberalism and Empire: A Study in Nineteenth-Century British Liberal Thought* (Chicago: University of Chicago Press, 1999).

9. Mary Louise Pratt, *Imperial Eyes: Travel Writing and Transculturation* (London: Routledge, 1992).

10. George W. Stocking Jr., *Victorian Anthropology* (New York: Free Press, 1987).

11. Frances E. Colenso, *History of the Zulu War and Its Origin: Assisted in Those Portions of the Work Which Touch upon Military Matters by Lieut.-Colonel Edward Durnford* (London: Chapman and Hall, 1880); idem, *The Ruin of Zululand: An Account of British Doings in Zululand since the Invasion of 1879—Being a Sequel to the History of the Zulu War, by Frances Ellen Colenso and Lieut.-Colonel Edward Durnford* (London: Ridgway, 1884).

12. E. D. Morel, *King Leopold's Rule in Africa* (London: Heinemann, 1904); idem, *Red Rubber: The Story of The Rubber Slave Trade Flourishing in the Congo in the Year of Grace 1906* (London: Unwin, 1907).

13. David Walker, *Appeal to the Coloured Citizens of the World, but in Particular, and Very Expressly, to Those of the United States of America* (Boston, 1830), 31.

14. "Fellow citizens, above your national, tumultuous joy, I hear the mournful wail of millions! Whose chains, heavy and grievous yesterday, are, today, rendered more intolerable by the jubilee shouts that reach them. If I do forget, if I do not faithfully remember those bleeding children of sorry this day, 'may my right hand cleave to the roof of my mouth'! To forget them, to pass lightly over their wrongs, and to chime in with the popular theme would be treason most scandalous and shocking, and would make me a reproach before God and the world. My subject, then, fellow citizens, is American slavery. I shall see this day and its popular characteristics from the slave's point of view. Standing there identified with the American bond-

man, making his wrongs mine. I do not hesitate to declare with all my soul that the character and conduct of this nation never looked blacker to me than on this Fourth of July! Whether we turn to the declarations of the past or to the professions of the present, the conduct of the nation seems equally hideous and revolting. America is false to the past, false to the present, and solemnly binds herself to be false to the future. Standing with God and the crushed and bleeding slave on this occasion, I will, in the name of humanity which is outraged, in the name of liberty which is fettered, in the name of the Constitution and the Bible which are disregarded and trampled upon, dare to call in question and to denounce, with all the emphasis I can command, everything that serves to perpetuate slavery—the great sin and shame of America!" "What to the Slave Is the Fourth of July?" 5 July 1852; originally published as a pamphlet, and included in James M. Gregory, *Frederick Douglass, the Orator: Containing an Account of His Life, His Eminent Public Services, His Brilliant Career as Orator, Selections from His Speeches and Writings* (Springfield, Mass.: Willey, 1893), 103–106. Text at afgen.com/douglas.html.

15. Ibid.

16. Angelina Emily Grimké, *Appeal to the Christian Women of the South* (New York: Arno, 1969; orig. pub. 1836), 3.

17. Angelina Emily Grimké, "Human Rights Not Founded on Sex," in Grimké, *Letters to Catherine Beecher* (Boston: Isaac Knapp, 1838), letter 12.

18. James Baldwin, "Everybody's Protest Novel," in Baldwin, *Notes of a Native Son* (London: Corgi, 1965), 10.

19. Costas Douzinas, *Human Rights and Empire: The Political Philosophy of Cosmopolitanism* (Abington, U.K.: Routledge-Cavendish, 2007). Sigmund Freud, *The Standard Edition of the Complete Psychological Works, Volume 17: 1917–1919*, trans. and ed. James Strachey (London: Hogarth, 1958), 180.

20. Luc Boltanski, *Distant Suffering: Morality, Media, and Politics*, trans. Graham Burchell (Cambridge: Cambridge University Press, 1999).

21. Hannah Arendt, "Reflections on Little Rock," *Dissent*, 6 (1959): 45–56; Vikki Bell, *Feminist Imagination: Genealogies in Feminist Theory* (London: Sage, 1999), ch. 4; Danielle Allen, "Law's Necessary Forcefulness: Ralph Ellison and Hannah Arendt on the Battle of Little Rock," in Anthony Simon

Laden and David Owen, eds., *Multiculturalism and Political Theory* (Cambridge: Cambridge University Press, 2007).

22. Dora Apel and Shawn Michelle Smith, *Lynching Photographs* (Berkeley: University of California Press and the Getty Foundation, 2007).

23. Ida B. Wells-Barnett, "A Red Record: Tabulated Statistics and Alleged Causes of Lynchings in the United States" (1895), in Wells-Barnett, *Selected Writings,* ed. Trudier Harris (Oxford: Oxford University Press, 1991), 217.

24. Joseph E. Harris, *African-American Reactions to War in Ethiopia, 1936–1941* (Baton Rouge: Louisiana State University Press, 1994); William R. Scott, *Sons of Sheba's Race: African Americans and the Italo-Ethiopian War, 1935–1941* (Bloomington: University of Indiana Press, 1993).

25. Rainer Baudendistel, *Between Bombs and Good Intentions: The Red Cross and the Italo-Ethiopian War, 1935–1936* (New York: Berghahn, 2006).

26. Antoine Frangulis, "Address of M. Frangulis, Delegate of Haiti, before the Plenary Assembly," *Official Journal of the League of Nations,* special supplement, no. 115 (1933).

27. Jan Herman Burgers, "The Road to San Francisco: The Revival of the Human Rights Idea in the Twentieth Century," *Human Rights Quarterly,* 14, no. 4 (November 1992): 447–477; A. W. Brian Simpson, *Human Rights and the End of Empire: Britain and the Genesis of the European Convention* (Oxford: Oxford University Press, 2001), esp. ch. 3; Paul Gordon Lauren, *The Evolution of International Human Rights: Visions Seen,* 2nd ed. (Philadelphia: University of Pennsylvania Press, 2003).

28. Du Bois, Gandhi, Voegelin, Arendt, Levinas, Sartre, Fanon, Foucault, Agamben.

29. Jeffrey Brainard, "U.S. Defense Secretary Asks Universities for New Cooperation," *Chronicle of Higher Education,* April 16, 2008, chronicle.com/news/article/4316/us-defense-secretary-asks-universities-for-new-cooperation (accessed May 16, 2009).

30. Giorgio Agamben, *Homo Sacer: Sovereign Power and Bare Life,* trans. Daniel Heller-Roazen (Stanford, Calif.: Stanford University Press, 1998), 166.

31. Jean Améry, "The Birth of Man from the Spirit of Violence: Frantz

Fanon the Revolutionary," trans. Adrian Daub, *Wasafiri*, 44 (Spring 2005): 13–18.

32. Primo Levi, *The Drowned and the Saved*, trans. Raymond Rosenthal (London: Picador, 1989).

33. The figure of the *Bettnachzieher* ("bed after-puller") is, in my reading of the text, Levi's cipher of this crowning race-friendly absurdity.

34. Raphael Patai, *The Arab Mind*, rev. ed. (New York: Hatherleigh, 2007; orig. pub. 1973); David Pryce-Jones, *The Closed Circle: An Interpretation of the Arabs* (London: Weidenfeld and Nicolson, 1989).

35. Walter Benjamin, "The Storyteller," in Benjamin, *Illuminations*, trans. Harry Zohn, ed. Hannah Arendt (London: Fontana, 1973), 94.

36. Richard Norton-Taylor, "SAS Man Quits in Protest at 'Illegal' Iraq War," *Guardian*, 13 March 2006.

37. This phrase is taken from W. E. B. Du Bois, who used the Latin *tertium quid*. See Du Bois, *The Souls of Black Folk* (Oxford: Oxford University Press, 2007; orig. pub. 1903), ch. 6.

38. Margaret Canovan, *Hannah Arendt: A Reinterpretation of Her Political Thought* (Cambridge: Cambridge University Press, 1992), 37. She is quoting Arendt's essay "The Political Meaning of Racial Anti-Semitism" (1946); see also Hannah Arendt, *The Origins of Totalitarianism*, 3rd ed. (London: Allen and Unwin, 1967), 436.

39. Arendt, *Origins of Totalitarianism*, 299.

40. Ibid., 300.

41. Emmanuel Levinas, "Reflections on the Philosophy of Hitlerism," trans. Sean Hand, *Critical Inquiry*, 17 (Autumn 1990): 71.

42. Sven Lindqvist, *A History of Bombing*, trans. Linda Haverty Rugg (New York: New Press, 2001). Carl Schmitt, *The Nomos of the Earth in the International Law of the Jus Publicum Europaeum*, trans. G. L. Ulmen (New York: Telos, 2003).

43. Nasser Hussain, *The Jurisprudence of Emergency: Colonialism and the Rule of Law* (Ann Arbor: University of Michigan Press, 2003).

44. Michael Taussig, "Culture of Terror—Space of Death: Roger Casement's Putumayo Report and the Explanation of Torture," *Comparative Studies in Society and History*, 26, no. 3 (1984): 467–49; idem, *Shamanism, Colo-*

nialism and the Wild Man: A Study in Terror and Healing (Chicago: University of Chicago Press, 1987).

45. Morel, *King Leopold's Rule in Africa;* idem, *Red Rubber;* Roger Casement, "The Putumayo Report," in Peter Singleton-Gates and Maurice Girodias, *The Black Diaries: An Account of Roger Casement's Life and Times, with a Collection of His Diaries and Public Writings* (Paris: Olympia, 1959), 220–309.

46. These words are taken from a 1956 radio interview which Sydney Rogers conducted in West Oakland several months after Parks's arrest.

47. Susan Buck-Morss, *Thinking Past Terror: Islamism and Critical Theory on the Left* (London: Verso, 2003), 93.

48. M. G. Smith, Roy Augier, and Rex Nettleford, *The Rastafari Movement in Kingston, Jamaica* (Mona, Jamaica: University College of the West Indies, 1960).

49. Wayne Perkins, interviewed by Jeremy Marre for the documentary film *Classic Albums: Bob Marley and the Wailers—Catch a Fire,* dir. Jeremy Marre (1999).

50. Vijay Prashad, *The Darker Nations: A People's History of the Third World* (New York: New Press, 2007); Robert J. C. Young, *Postcolonialism: An Historical Introduction* (Oxford: Blackwell, 2001).

51. *Melody Maker* (London), 2 June 1973, 25.

52. Richard Wright, *Twelve Million Black Voices* (London: Lindsay Drummond, 1947).

53. Brian Ward, *Just My Soul Responding: Rhythm and Blues, Black Consciousness and Race Relations* (London: University College of London Press, 1998).

54. Paul Gilroy, *There Ain't No Black in the Union Jack: The Cultural Politics of Race and Nation* (London: Routledge, 2002; orig. pub. 1987).

55. Cedella Booker, with Anthony Winkler, *Bob Marley: An Intimate Portrait by His Mother* (London: Viking Penguin, 1996).

56. Ibid., 103.

57. Ken Post, "The Bible as Ideology: Ethiopianism in Jamaica, 1930–1938," in Christopher Allen and R. W. Johnson, eds., *African Perspectives: Papers in the History, Politics and Economics of Africa Presented to Thomas Hodgkin* (Cambridge: Cambridge University Press, 1970), 185–207; Ken Post,

Arise Ye Starvelings: The Jamaican Labour Rebellion of 1938 and Its Aftermath (The Hague: Nijhoff, 1978).

58. Piero Gleijeses, *Conflicting Missions: Havana, Washington and Africa, 1959–1976* (Chapel Hill: University of North Carolina Press, 2002).

59. Aimé Césaire, *Discourse on Colonialism*, trans. Joan Pinkham (New York: Monthly Review Press, 1972).

60. *Melody Maker* (London), 2 June 1973, 25.

61. Frantz Fanon, *Black Skin, White Masks*, trans. Charles Lam Markmann (London: Pluto, 1986; orig. pub. 1967), 42.

62. Martin Luther King Jr., *Strength To Love* (New York: Harper and Row, 1963).

3. Troubadours, Warriors, and Diplomats

1. Alain Locke, *The Negro and His Music* (Washington, D.C.: Associates in Negro Folk Education, 1936), 4.

2. Penny Von Eschen, *Satchmo Blows Up the World: Jazz Ambassadors Play the Cold War* (Cambridge, Mass.: Harvard University Press, 2004).

3. Locke, *The Negro and His Music*, 99.

4. T. W. Adorno, "On the Fetish-Character in Music and the Regression of Listening," in Adorno, *Essays on Music*, ed. Richard Leppert (Berkeley: University of California Press, 2002, 1938), 288–818.

5. Laura Bush, remarks at press conference, 25 September 2006, www.whitehouse.gov/news/releases/2006/09/20060925-2.html. We saw art diplomacy during the Cold War, when even as the Soviet Union and the United States were on the brink of conflict, the people of these two countries found a common interest in jazz. Behind the Iron Curtain, Willis Conover, the Voice of America disk jockey, who announced *Music U.S.A. Jazz Hour* each week, was a hero to Soviet citizens. His broadcasts are said to have done more to improve U.S.-Soviet relations than any official negotiations could. Today, art has the same power to reduce tensions and strengthen alliances.

6. Caetano Veloso, *Tropical Truth: A Story of Music and Revolution in Brazil* (New York: Knopf, 2002), 168.

7. Albert King, "Blues at Sunrise," from the LP *Live Wire / Blues Power* (Stax Records STX-4128, undated).

8. Martin Luther King Jr., *Where Do We Go from Here: Chaos or Community?* (New York: Harper and Row, 1967), 57.

9. Ibid., 66.

10. This interview was originally part of Joe Boyd's 1973 documentary film *Hendrix*. It is transcribed and published in Ben Valkhoff, ed., *Eyewitness: The Illustrated Hendrix Concerts, 1968* (Rotterdam: Up from the Skies, 2000), 69.

11. Sadly, Experience Hendrix have denied me permission to quote the song here. The lyrics can, however, be easily located on the Web.

12. Noel Redding and Carol Appleby, *Are You Experienced? The Inside Story of the Jimi Hendrix Experience* (London: Fourth Estate, 1990), 21.

13. Eric Burdon, with J. Marshall Craig, *Don't Let Me Be Misunderstood* (New York: Thunder's Mouth Press / Avalon, 2002).

14. See Ernst Bloch's 1959 essay "Better Castles in the Sky at the Country Fair and Circus, in Fairy Tales and Colportage," reprinted in Bloch, *The Utopian Function of Art and Literature: Selected Essays,* trans. Jack Zipes and Frank Mecklenburg (Cambridge, Mass.: MIT Press, 1988), 167–185.

15. Herbert Marcuse, *Eros and Civilisation: A Philosophical Inquiry into Freud* (London: Abacus, 1969; orig. pub. 1955), 164.

16. Susan Sontag, "Model Destinations," *Times Literary Supplement,* 22 June 1984, 699–700.

17. Albert King, "The Blues Don't Change," from the LP *The Pinch* (Stax Records STX-3001, 1977).

18. Eric Hobsbawm, "Inventing Traditions," in Eric Hobsbawm and Terence Ranger, eds., *The Invention of Tradition* (Cambridge: Cambridge University Press, 1982), 2.

19. Richard Wright, *Twelve Million Black Voices* (London: Lindsay Drummond, 1947; orig. pub. 1941), 135.

20. Ibid., 146.

21. Ralph Ellison, "The Charlie Christian Story," in Ellison, *Shadow and Act* (New York: Random House, 1964), 234.

22. Ibid., 239.

23. Locke, *The Negro and His Music*, 90.

24. Nikolas Rose, *Inventing Our Selves: Psychology, Power, and Personhood* (Cambridge: Cambridge University Press, 1996), 37.

25. See Keith Shadwick, "Running the Voodoo Child Down," *Jazzwise*, 60 (December 2002–January 2003): 22–29.

26. "The single factor that drove me to practice was that sound I had heard from the Hawaiian or country-and-western steel pedal guitar. That cry sounded human to me. I wanted to sustain a note like a singer. I wanted to phrase a note like a sax player. By bending the strings, by trilling my hand—and I have big fat hands—I could achieve something that approximated a vocal vibrato; I could sustain a note. I wanted to connect my guitar to human emotions: by fooling with the feedback between amplifier and instrument, I started experimenting with sounds that expressed my feelings, whether happy or sad, bouncy or bluesy. I was looking for ways to let my guitar sing." B. B. King, with David Ritz, *The Blues All Around Me: The Autobiography of B. B. King* (London: Hodder and Stoughton, 1996), 123.

27. Ralph Ellison, interviewed by Robert Penn Warren, in Warren, *Who Speaks for the Negro?* (New York: Vintage 1966), 327.

28. Barack Obama, *Dreams from My Father*, 2nd ed. (Edinburgh: Canongate, 2007), vii.

29. Edition.cnn.com/2005/POLITICS/09/13/katrina.rice (accessed May 7, 2009).

30. Raphael Patai, *The Arab Mind* (London: Macmillan, 1983). See also Frances S. Hasso, "'Culture Knowledge' and the Violence of Imperialism: Revisiting the Arab Mind," web.mit.edu/cis/www/mitejmes/issues/2007sp /CULTURE%20KNOWLEDGE-%20Hasso.pdf (accessed May 7, 2009).

31. Ian Hacking, *Historical Ontology* (Cambridge, Mass.: Harvard University Press, 2002).

32. Frantz Fanon, "Racism and Culture," in Fanon, *Toward the African Revolution: Political Essays*, trans. Haakon Chevalier (New York: Monthly Review, 1967), 44.

33. See, for example, the text of President Bush's speech to the annual NAACP convention on 20 July 2006: www.washingtonpost.com/wp-dyn

/content/article/2006/07/20/AR2006072000803.html (accessed May 22, 2009).

34. Www.guardian.co.uk/world/2008/mar/28/barackobama.uselections 20081 (accessed May 7, 2009).

35. James Clifford, *Routes: Travel and Translation in the Late Twentieth Century* (Cambridge, Mass.: Harvard University Press, 1997).

36. U.S. Department of State, *Cultural Diplomacy, the Linchpin of Public Diplomacy: Report of the Advisory Committee on Cultural Diplomacy* (Washington, D.C., September 2005).

37. Pew Global Attitudes Project, "A Sixteen-Nation Pew Global Attitudes Survey," June 2005, www.pewglobal.org.

38. A small but telling measure of the global resonance of that campaign for the presidency can be gleaned from the Mighty Sparrow's 2008 CD *Barack de Magnificent* (BLSCD1050) and Cocoa Tea's Jamaican hit song "Barack Obama" (Roaring Lion Records, 2008). Many other similar recordings have been produced throughout the world.

39. This phrase is Benjamin Barber's; see Barber, *Jihad vs. McWorld* (New York: Times Books, 1995). See also Jeff Fleischer, "Operation Hollywood: How the Pentagon Bullies Movie Producers into Showing the U.S. Military in the Best Possible Light," *Mother Jones,* 20 September 2004.

40. Susan Buck-Morss, *Thinking Past Terror: Islamism and Critical Theory on the Left* (London: Verso, 2004).

41. The torturers' taste in tunes is questionable. Springsteen's "Born in the U.S.A.," for example, has been a favourite in the secret prisons, repeating the mistake made by the Reagan campaign in 1984, when the Republicans thought the chorus—"Born in the U.S.A.!"—would make a campaign chant for loyalists. Yet the message of the song is harshly critical of American policy, condemning the war in Vietnam and describing a veteran's efforts to find work.

Other lyrics used by today's torturers seem equally inappropriate. In "White America," Eminem raps that he plans to "piss on the lawns of the White House" and "spit liquor in the faces of this democracy of hypocrisy." It is difficult to see how President Bush could approve of this, let alone the verse where Eminem expresses his intention to have sex with the vice president's wife. Clive Stafford Smith, "Torture by Music," *New Statesman and Society,* 6 November 2006, www.newstatesman.com/writers/clive_stafford _smith/page/3 (accessed May 22, 2009). See also www.youtube.com /watch?v=ZKoghRXzbYw.

42. See www.commondreams.org/headlines04/0417-17.htm (accessed May 15, 2009).

43. Jan Melissen, ed., *The New Public Diplomacy: Soft Power in International Relations* (Basingstoke, U.K.: Palgrave Macmillan, 2007).

44. Sigmund Freud, "Disillusionment in Times of War," in Freud, *The Standard Edition of the Complete Psychological Works, Volume 14: 1914–1916,* trans. and ed. James Strachey (London: Hogarth, 1958). George Orwell, *Orwell and Politics: Animal Farm in the Context of Essays, Reviews and Letters Selected from the Complete Works of George Orwell,* ed. Peter Davison (London: Penguin, 2001). Edward Bernays, *Propaganda* (New York: Liveright, 1928).

45. David Rohde, "Army Enlists Anthropology in War Zones," *New York Times,* 5 October 2007, www.nytimes.com/2007/10/05/world/asia/05afghan .html. David Glenn, "Anthropologists in a War Zone: Scholars Debate Their Role," *Chronicle of Higher Education,* 30 November 2007, chronicle.com /free/v54/i14/14a00101.htm. BBC News, "New Media Plan to Combat Taleban," 10 October 2008, newsvote.bbc.co.uk/mpapps/pagetools/print/news .bbc.co.uk/1/hi/uk/7662549.stm (all URLs here accessed May 22, 2009).

46. This process has been given the useful name "agnotology" by the historians Robert Proctor and Londa Schiebinger. See Proctor and Schiebinger, eds., *Agnotology: The Making and Unmaking of Ignorance* (Stanford, Calif.: Stanford University Press, 2008).

47. Bobbie Johnson, "U.S. Military Unveils Its Answer to YouTube: TroopTube," *The Guardian,* 12 November 2008.

48. Jared Cohen, *Children of Jihad: A Young American's Travels among the Youth of the Middle East* (New York: Gotham/Penguin, 2007), 273–274.

49. James Yee, with Aimee Molloy, *For God and Country: Faith and Patriotism under Fire* (New York: Public Affairs Press, 2005).

50. Janis Karpinski, with Steven Strasser, *One Woman's Army: The Commanding General of Abu Ghraib Tells Her Story* (New York: Hyperion, 2005), 219.

51. "I think the lesson . . . [is] to look at al-Qaeda primarily as a propaganda hub. What bin Laden is trying to be is not the Commander-in-Chief, but the Inciter-in-Chief. What he's trying to do is to provoke the West into actions that basically incite the *umma*, the world's Muslim population, into a mass revolt and a mass movement. And that's why I think it's appropriate to see al-Qaeda as fundamentally an insurgent movement rather than a terrorist movement." From an interview with the preeminent theorist of global counter-insurgency, David Kilcullen, conducted by Frank Gardner and broadcast on *Analysis*, BBC Radio 4, 1 November 2007. See news.bbc.co.uk/nol/shared/spl/hi/programmes/analysis/transcripts/01_11_07.txt (accessed May 22, 2009).

52. President Bush's acknowledgement of the history of racism at the 2006 annual convention of the NAACP should be understood in this light.

53. Richard Norton-Taylor and Jamie Wilson, "U.S. Army in Iraq Institutionally Racist, Claims British Officer," *The Guardian*, 12 January 2006.

54. Pew Research Center, "Blacks See Growing Values Gap between Poor and Middle Class: Optimism about Black Progress Declines," 13 November 2007, pewresearch.org/pubs/634/black-public-opinion.

55. "Hip Hop inside Iraq: Soldiers' Stories," *The Source*, 227 (November 2008); Karen Gilchrist, "Soldier Rapper Tells His Tale of Iraq," BBC News, 22 March 2006, news.bbc.co.uk/2/hi/americas/4828816.stm. See also Scott Johnson and Eve Conant, "Soldier Rap, the Pulse of War," *Newsweek*, 13 June 2005, www.newsweek.com/id/50076 (both URLs accessed May 22, 2009).

56. Whitney Joiner, "The Army Be Thuggin' It," www.salon.com/mwt/feature/2003/10/17/army/print.html (accessed May 22, 2009).

57. Phenomics is the study of genomic information in order to better understand the complex relationship between genotype (the genetic makeup of an individual) and phenotype (the observable traits of an individual).

Acknowledgements

I have become wary of publicly thanking my ex-students, because they have too often been unfairly made responsible for my political and scholarly deviations. I would like to take this opportunity to emphasise that my errors are my own responsibility. Having made that confession, my heartfelt gratitude goes to Dr. Radiclani Clytus, especially, for his beyond-the-call assistance with the journal *Human Rights* and the life of Elizur Wright. I thank Dr. Anthony Foy for introducing me to a particularly inspiring image of Jack Johnson behind the wheel. In no particular order, I am also grateful to Bogdan State, Dr. Jayna Brown, Dr. Ivy Wilson, Dr. Lucia Trimbur, Dr. Louise Bernard, Dr. Josh Guild, Dr. Mary Barr, Dr. Emmanuel Tipsarevic, and Dr. Hiroki Ogasawara for the various forms of help and support they have furnished me. Omar El Khairy, Richard Bramwell, Leah Mancina Khaghani, and Monia Wadham are also all part of this book in one way or another.

I thank my colleagues past and present, especially Hazel Carby, Michael Veal, Alondra Nelson, John Szwed, Les Back, Dick Hobbs, Nikolas Rose, Suki Ali, and Nicolas Guilhot.

With regard to this particular project, I am also endebted to Ed

Vulliamy, Gary Younge, Rip Lhamon, Angela McRobbie, Tom Zacharias, Colin MacCabe, Isaac Julien, Jean-Paul Bourelly, David A. Bailey, Miguel Melino, Robert JFC Young, Jill Lewis, Hedda Ekerwald, Anthony Barnett, Achille Mbembe, and LKJ for their help, dialogue, and friendship.

The luthiers Jack Briggs (North Carolina) and Chris George (Lincolnshire) have helped me to realize more of my sonic dreams. Shinichiro Suzuki is thanked for a minty-fresh replacement copy of Peter Tosh's "Babylon Queendom" (Intel-diplo), which along with Dennis Brown's "Running Up and Down" distills the metatext of these scribblings.

Cora Hatshepsut Gilroy Ware and Marcus Gilroy Ware are bigged up here above all for their curiosity, their example, their energy, and their unwavering faith in the future.

Semper Vron.

Peace out.

Index